DAVE
HOM

INSI

- **How**
  Look for that intangible quality called "professionalism" (a.k.a. "car size") because you'll spend most of your time in that car looking at homes you cannot afford.

- **How to interpret real estate ads**
  "Charming" can mean "toilets that flush up."

- **Helpful packing hints**
  It is best not to pack important prescription drugs such as tranquilizers. It is best to keep them on hand and gulp them down like salted peanuts.

- **How to redecorate for under $650,000**
  A small carpet stain where the cat vomited in 1979 can be made to "disappear" when company comes by having a predetermined family member stand on it and refuse to move.

- **And much more!**

By Dave Barry:

DAVE BARRY'S GUIDE TO MARRIAGE AND/OR
  SEX
CLAW YOUR WAY TO THE TOP
STAY FIT AND HEALTHY 'TIL YOU'RE DEAD
BABIES AND OTHER HAZARDS OF SEX
TAMING OF THE SCREW
BAD HABITS: A 100% FACT-FREE BOOK
DAVE BARRY SLEPT HERE*
DAVE BARRY TURNS 40*
DAVE BARRY TALKS BACK
DAVE BARRY'S ONLY TRAVEL GUIDE YOU'LL
  EVER NEED*
DAVE BARRY DOES JAPAN*
DAVE BARRY IS NOT MAKING THIS UP*
DAVE BARRY'S HOMES AND OTHER BLACK
  HOLES

*Published by Ballantine Books

DAVE BARRY'S HOMES AND OTHER BLACK HOLES

The Happy Homeowner's Guide to Ritual Closing Ceremonies, Newton's First Law of Furniture Buying, the Lethal Chemicals Man, and Other Perils of the American Dream

Dave Barry

Illustrated by Jeff MacNelly

BALLANTINE BOOKS • NEW YORK

This book contains an excerpt from the upcoming hardcover edition of *Dave Barry's Complete Guide to Guys* by Dave Barry. This excerpt has been set for this edition only and may not reflect the final content of the hardcover edition.

Copyright © 1988 by Dave Barry
Illustrations copyright © by Jeff MacNelly
Excerpt copyright © 1995 by Dave Barry

All rights reserved under International and Pan-American Copyright Conventions. Published in the United States by Ballantine Books, a division of Random House, Inc., New York, and simultaneously in Canada by Random House of Canada Limited, Toronto.

Library of Congress Catalog Card Number: 87-91406

ISBN 0-345-39440-2

Manufactured in the United States of America

First Trade Edition: September 1988
First Mass Market Edition: May 1995

10 9 8 7 6 5 4 3 2 1

Contents

INTRODUCTION

Why It Was Probably a Mistake to Buy This Book

The desire to own a home of one's own has been a part of human nature ever since that fateful moment, millions of years ago, when our earliest ancestors climbed down out of their trees and moved into their very first caves. It was a major moment in history, and its glory was dimmed only slightly by

First Cave

First Furniture Arrives for First Cave

the fact that their furniture did not arrive for another 250,000 years.

Yes, moving into a new home is one of life's great adventures, constantly posing new and exciting challenges.

For example, just recently my wife, son, and I moved to Florida, and the first thing I noticed was that there were crabs living under our house. There were two main ones, named Bob and Steve, who had established holes on either side of our front door, which they were always working on. I'd come out in the morning to get the paper, and there would be Bob and Steve, waving their claws at me as if to say in cheerful crab language: "Hi, Mr. Barry! We're digging holes under your house, and unless you do something, the entire structure will eventually fall into the canal!"

What I ultimately decided to do about the crabs was the same thing I ultimately do about virtually all homeowner-type problems, namely—and you might want to write this down, because it is the core philosophy of this entire book—I try not to think about it. Trust me, this is the best way. If God had wanted us to spend all our time fretting

Essential tools you will need for homeowner-type problems:

Beer   Glass   Chair

about the problems of home ownership, He would never have created beer.

This is not to say that I am recommending that you totally ignore your responsibilities as a homeowner and just sit around all day with a beer can in your hand. No indeed, I have long been a believer in purchasing bottled beer, and pouring it into a chilled glass. "If you're going to do something, do it right"—that is my motto, and you will find that throughout this book I have made every effort to present all relevant houseowning information as accurately and completely as possible given the fact that I am making almost all of it up.

Which is not to say that I am unqualified to write this book. I have bought and sold several homes in my day, although I will admit that in the case of our current home, I never even saw it until after I signed the agreement of sale. My wife, Beth, did the actual shopping. This is because I get extremely nervous in sales situations. I will do absolutely anything to please the salesperson. Usually, in stores, I can flee on foot before a salesperson gets to me, but if I don't get away, I'm a dead man. Like, if I'm walking through Sears, and I happen to pause for just a moment in the major appliances section, and one of those Sears appliance salespersons in polyester sport jackets comes sidling up and says, "Can I help you?" I instantly go into a state of extreme anxiety and say: "Yes, I'll take one of these, please," pointing to whatever major appliance I happen to be standing in front of, even though we probably already have one.

So I am a bad person to have on your side in a real estate sales situation. I drive my wife crazy, because I always want to buy whatever structure we happen to be standing in:

ME: Well! This looks perfect!
MY WIFE: This is the real estate broker's office.
ME: Well, how much are they asking?

This is why I was not actively involved in the purchase of our present house. But I still have to help pay for it, which is why even though *you* may not be thrilled that you bought this book, *I'm* certainly glad you did.

1

Getting Ready to Get
Real Depressed

DECIDING WHICH HOUSE TO BUY

In deciding which house to buy, the first
thing you have to do is determine your Price
Range, using this simple formula:

1. Take your total annual family income, including coins that have fallen behind the

bureau and any projected future revenue you have been notified about via personalized letters from Mr. Ed McMahon stating that you may already have won fourteen million dollars.

2. Count up the number of children you have and note how many of them are named Joshua or Ashley. That many? Really? Don't you feel this trend toward giving children designer names has gone far enough? Don't you think we should go back to the old system of naming children after beloved uncles and aunts, even if we in fact hate our beloved uncles and aunts and they have comical names such as Lester? Can you imagine having an aunt named Lester? These questions are not directly related to your Price Range. I'm just curious to know how you feel.

3. Now take these figures (No! I'm *not* going to tell you again which ones! Pay attention!) and multiply them by six; which will tell you, in thousands of yards, roughly how far away the lightning bolt was. No! Wait! Sorry! Wrong formula! You want to take these figures and multiply them by something *other* than six.

2

This should give you a very strong idea of what your Price Range is, although we shall soon see that it doesn't matter because there are no homes in it anyway.

There! Now you're getting somewhere! But you're not done yet: you need to decide what style of house you're looking for. The major styles of houses in the United States are:

- OLDER HOUSES with many quaint and charming architectural features such as that during certain phases of the moon the toilets flush up.
- NEWER HOUSES built by large developers using modern cost-cutting efficiency measures such as hiring semiskilled derelict felon gypsy work-persons who are prone to forgetting to install key architectural elements such as windows and those large pieces of wood, "rafters" I believe they are called, that hold up the roof.
- REALLY NICE WELL-BUILT, WELL-LOCATED, AFFORDABLE HOUSES that are not for sale.

Another very important factor is neighborhood. Ask any real estate broker to name the three most important factors in buying a property, and he'll say: "Location, location, location." Now ask him to name the chief justice of the United States Supreme Court, and he'll say: "Location, location, location." This tells us that we should not necessarily be paying a whole lot of attention to real estate brokers.

If you have school-age children, by far the most important factor in selecting a neighborhood is, of course, the proximity of the nearest Toys Backwards "R" Us store. You will be spending a great deal of your time and disposable income there, because from kindergarten through about sixth grade, the average child attends approximately 36,500 birthday parties. Your child will go through a period, usually around first grade, when his classmates will have as many as six birthdays apiece per year, meaning you'll spend virtually all of your Saturdays racing to Toys Backwards "R" Us, then racing off to the party, leaving a trail of flattened pedestrians because you are wrapping the present as you drive. But all the hassle is worth it when you see the look on the birthday child's face when he or she rips open the present and remarks with delight: "Hey! I already *got* this!"

Location, location, location.

Once you have selected several potential neighborhoods, you should drive around to evaluate them, using this convenient . . .

Good

Bad

Neighborhood Checklist

Note What the Residents Do with Cars That No Longer Function

—Good Neighborhood: They get rid of them.

—Bad Neighborhood: They keep them all forever, arranged tastefully on their lawns, as if expecting the Car Fairy to come one night and whisk all the cars away and leave everybody a nice shiny quarter.

Note What Kind of Names the Local Streets Have

—Good: Jasmine View Court Terrace

—Bad: Interstate 95

Note What Kind of Businesses Are Operating In the Neighborhood

—Good: Arthur A. Wutherington IV, Investment Banker

—Bad: Earl's All-Night Nude Revue & Motorcycle Repair

Note What the Neighborhood Youths Are Doing

—Good: Selling lemonade

—Bad: Selling you your rear wheels back

Good

Bad

Note What Kind of Bumper Stickers the Neighborhood Cars Have
—Good: "SCHOOL'S OPEN! DRIVE CAREFULLY!"
—Bad: "I ♥ MY PIT BULL"

Bumper Stickers in your neighborhood:

Good

Bad

Worse

Note the Types of Neighborhood Social Activities

—Good: Barbecues

—Bad: Cockfights

It also might be a good idea to do some formal research into neighborhood property values by going down to the Municipal Building and getting shunted from one civil servant to another in an increasingly desperate attempt to find one who is not hostile, brain-damaged, or eating lunch, until finally you open fire at random with a semiautomatic weapon. So we can see that this is not, after all, such a good idea, and it probably should not even be included here. Although frankly I doubt that any jury in the land would convict you.

CHOOSING A REAL ESTATE BROKER

It is possible to buy or sell a home without a broker, as will be discussed in a later chapter.*

*Unless we forget to write it.

But most people prefer to use a broker, because of the many advantages, such as:

Good Broker

Bad Broker

1. If you have a real estate broker, you have an excuse to fend off the other brokers, who will otherwise follow you around and hurl rocks through your window with notes taped to them explaining the many advantages of using a broker.
2. Brokers always have nicer cars than you do, a phenomenon that will become more

understandable when we get to the section on commissions.

This is by no means meant to be a comprehensive list of the advantages of using a broker. The only reason I'm not listing all the others here is that they don't spring immediately to mind.

The best place to obtain a broker is at a junior high school, where you'll find that virtually all the teachers obtained real estate licenses once they realized what a tragic mistake they had made, selecting a profession that requires them to spend entire days confined in small rooms with adolescent children. Often it is sufficient to just drive by the school and beep your horn; within seconds, brokers will come swarming out of doors and windows, eager to abandon their lesson plans on the Three Major Bones of the Inner Ear so they can help you find a home.

There are many factors to consider in selecting a broker, such as competence, honesty, vertical leap, and placement in the Evening Gown Competition. But the most important factor is an intangible quality called "professionalism," by which I mean "car size." You want to select the broker with the largest possible car, because you're going to spend far more time in this car than in whatever home you ultimately buy.

Next you should tell your broker what your Price Range is, so he or she can laugh until his or her official company blazer is soaked with drool. What your broker finds so amusing, of course, is that there is virtually nothing, outside of the Third World, available in your Price Range. I don't care if your Price Range is a hillion jillion dollars, there will be nothing available in it. This is a fundamental principle of real estate.

At first you will probably insist on looking at the something in your Price Range anyway, which will result in the following comical dialogue:

YOU: This is *it*? They're asking $89,500 for a *refrigerator carton*?

BROKER: Yes, but I think they'll take $85,000.

This process is called "getting a feel for the market." Once you've undergone it, your

broker will explain a creative new financial
concept that has been developed to enable
people such as yourself to enjoy the benefits
of home ownership, called: Spending Way
More Than You Can Afford. Usually you
have to talk yourself into going with this
concept. Here are some sound financial ar-
guments you can use:

1. Although you may not really be able to
   afford a more expensive home at your
   current income level, it makes sense to
   buy it anyway, because in just a few
   years, at your current rate of progress in
   your career, you'll probably be dead.
2. There are major *tax benefits* to owning a
   home. The law, written by wise lawyers
   and bankers, permits you to deduct all
   the money you give to lawyers or bankers, which will turn out to be virtually all
   the money you have.
3. Owning a home is a *smart investment*. As
   inflation pushes up the cost of living, you
   will build up equity[1] in your home, so

[1]Mysterious kind of money that everybody is always
claiming belongs to you, even though you never actually

that, when you eventually sell it, you will have made enough profit to be able to afford to pay the points[2] and closing costs[3] on your next home!

So as you can see, you really can't afford *not* to buy a home that you really can't afford. It's time to sit down with your broker and take a serious look at the listings.

The listings are computerized lists, or "listings," of all the houses that all the brokers in your region have been trying to sell since the Carter administration. Listings are always written in a special real estate code. For example, this listing:

CHARMING[1] RANCH[2]—4BR[3] 3B[4] 2TD,[5] fully landscaped,[6] newly renovated.[7]

... can be decoded as follows:

1. Rooms the size of nasal spray cartons
2. IN URBAN AREAS: No attic or basement. IN RURAL AREAS: Also cattle have wintered in the foyer.

see it.

[2] Money you give to bankers so they will lend you money.

[3] Money you give to lawyers for no apparent reason.

15

3. Four bedrooms
4. Three bathrooms
5. Two turtle doves
6. Extensive comical lawn statuary including minority groups holding lanterns; also large, permanent, fully mechanized, spectacularly illuminated display of Santa's Workshop
7. The walls have been pretty well scraped clean in the room where the demonic beings from another dimension came through the TV set and caused the previous occupants' heads to explode.

Study the listings carefully and make a note of any houses that look right for you, so your broker can confirm that they were all sold just that morning. This is actually good, because it will help to get you into the proper highly desperate frame of mind where you will do almost anything to get a house, including paying large sums of money you really don't have to people you really don't know for reasons you really aren't sure of. Which is the essence of real estate.

2

How to Pretend to Look Knowledgeably at Houses

Okay. Now we have reached the most exciting part, the very essence of home buying: actually going inside specific houses so we can examine them and fail to notice major defects.

One important warning before you get started: You want to be on the alert for the Helpful Seller. This is the kind of seller who,

The helpful seller.

the instant you enter his home, leaps out and attaches himself to you, like an intestinal parasite, only worse, because intestinal parasites, for all their flaws, do not feel a great need to point out every single one of their home's numerous features, whereas the Helpful Seller does.

18

"This is the hall bathroom," he'll say, showing you a bathroom in a hall. Then he'll watch you very closely, trying to gauge your reaction to this bathroom, and you'll feel obligated to *compliment* him on it.

"Very nice!" you'll say.

"This toilet seat was installed quite recently," he'll say.

"Huh!" you'll say.

"It's padded," he'll say.

"Bang," you'll say, shooting him in the forehead with your small-caliber revolver. This is why many real estate brokers these days use tranquilizer darts to subdue hyperactive sellers right in the foyer, before they have a chance to become too Helpful.

HOW MANY HOUSES SHOULD YOU LOOK AT?

Most experts recommend that, for maximum effectiveness, you should look at forty-five or even fifty houses per day. Experienced home shoppers often reach the point where they can leap out of the real estate broker's car, look at a house, and get back into the car before it reaches a complete stop.

If you follow this procedure, by nightfall your brain will be tightly packed with hundreds of thousands of bits of important real estate information, and you and your spouse will be able to have useful decision-making conversations like this:

YOU: I kind of liked that contemporary with the fireplace in the kitchen.

YOUR SPOUSE: No, the contemporary had fire *damage* in the kitchen. You're thinking of the split-level, the one where the garage floor had a Rust-Oleum stain shaped like the Virgin Mary.

YOU: No, that was the colonial, remember? With big white pillars out front and no toilets?

YOUR SPOUSE: No, you're thinking of Monticello. Remember? We went there on vacation in 1979?

YOU: No, it was 1978.

Using this logical elimination process, you'll begin to narrow your list down to the three or four dozen houses that you are truly interested in. These are the ones you should go back and inspect in a thorough manner, using this convenient checklist:

HOME INSPECTION CHECKLIST

The Roof

This is a "must." There is an old German expression that goes: "A house without a roof is like a machterstrassefurtermorgennacht-dankeschoen without a gutsprechenbuch-lungwiegehtvolkswagenporsche." If anything, this is an understatement. So the first thing you should do is go up and crouch in the attic and see if you get bit by a bat. This is usually an indication that the house contains bats, which, depending on your lifestyle, could be a negative factor, especially if one tries to suck out your blood, because that means it's a vampire bat, which means the house is located in South America, so right away we are talking about probably a fairly long commute to work.

Also while you're up there you should look around and see if you notice any of the following important house parts:

The Attic

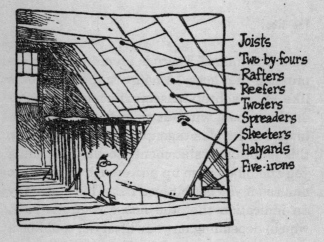

- Joists
- Two-by-fours
- Rafters
- Reefers
- Twofers
- Spreaders
- Skeeters
- Halyards
- Five-irons

You will recognize these objects instantly, because most of them are pieces of wood. Make a note of them.

The Floors

These should be sturdy and level. The only proven way to check for sturdiness is to drop a men's standard sixteen-pound bowling ball (*Always* carry one with you!) onto the floor from a height of seventy-five feet through a hole drilled in the roof, then carefully note the results. (No, the seller will not object, unless he has "something to hide.")

To check for levelness, you will need a standard piece of string and a standard rock. Using a standard knot, tie one end of the string, then, holding the *other* end of the string, stand in the middle of a room, and carefully note which way the rock points. Ideally, it will point toward the floor. If it points somewhere else, such as toward a wall, this is often an indication of nonlevelness (SEE DIAGRAM).

The Plumbing

Forget about the plumbing. It will work perfectly. It always does, when you inspect it, because plumbing is one of the most intelli-

Testing for levelness:

Level →

Not Level →

gent life forms on the planet, and it would never be so foolish as to tip its hand to you. It will wait until *after* you have bought the house. Then it will make its move. Late some night, you'll hear strange gurglings and sloshings in your pipes; this will be the sound of your toilets communicating with each other, making their plans:

FIRST TOILET: It's on. Tomorrow is New Year's Day, they have house guests, it's four degrees below zero outside, and their plumber is in Switzerland. We break tonight.

SECOND TOILET: Ha ha! I'll tell the hot water heater.

The Electrical System

The most important thing to find out about the electrical system is whether it contains enough "volts," which are little tiny pieces of energy shaped like arrows so you can tell which direction they're moving in science class diagrams, as shown on page 27.

The standard measurement for volts is "amps," also called "watts," which travel around in what is called a "circuit." A typical circuit works as follows:

At the electrical company, fuel oil is burned to set fire to a generator, which gives off electrical energy in the form of sparks, which are put into wires and sent to your home, where the electricity waits in the wall until you turn on your toaster, at which point it rushes through the wire and into the English muffin, and from there into your stomach, where it remains until a cool, dry day when you are walking down a hall scuffing your feet on a carpet and you go to open a door, causing the electricity to leap into the doorknob, where it remains forever, building up over time to tremendously high levels, which is why scientists are now concerned that if some unscrupulous entity such as Libya or God forbid an adolescent male ever figures how to release the power, he could, using only the latent doorknob energy contained in a single older ranch-style home, vaporize Oregon.

But your immediate concern, as a potential buyer, is making sure that the house has the right number of volts. Following is a chart depicting the most popular voltages currently available in the housing market:

POPULAR HOME VOLTAGES

120
220
9*

*Requires 9 volt battery (not included)

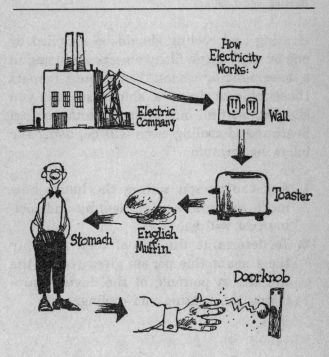

27

Which voltage is right for you? This, more than anything else, is a matter of personal taste; and like most matters of personal taste, it is best left in the hands of a qualified interior designer.

Heating and Cooling

Heating and cooling should be supplied by one or more large filthy objects squatting in a basement or closet. You should inspect these objects from a safe distance; you should also find out what the total annual heating and cooling costs will be, using the following formula:

1. Ask the person selling the house how much the total annual heating and cooling cost will be.
2. To determine the actual cost, multiply the amount this person gives you by the weight, in pounds, of the devices supplying the heating and cooling.

Insects

Make no mistake about it: there will be insects in the house. The entire planet is teeming with insect life; scientists now estimate that there are over 60,000,000,000,-000,000,000 different species living under my kitchen sink alone.

Fortunately, most insects pose no threat to homeowners. All they want is to eat your food and have babies in your sock drawer and maybe crawl up your nostril while you're sleeping. In exchange for this, many of them gladly perform useful household services, such as pooping on your toothbrush. "You scratch my back, and I'll suck blood out of yours"—that is the insect motto.

The exception, of course, is termites, which are small socialist insects that eat houses. (We don't know what they ate before houses were invented. We think maybe garages.) Termites live in large colonies ruled by a lady termite with an enormous butt, called the Queen, who governs over a strict termite hierarchy consisting of: the Biters, the Chewers, the Spit Makers, the Soldiers, the House of Commons, the Nannies, and the Cute Little Baby Eggs. Each of these colony members has specific duties and responsibilities that are clearly posted on the Bulletin Board, although of course, being insects, they are much too stupid to remember what these duties and responsibilities are, so they basically just scurry around at random. Nevertheless, as I noted earlier, they can eat your prospective house, so it is very important that you inspect carefully for the Two Telltale Signs of Termite Infestation, which are:

1. Termites walking around with pieces of your prospective house in their mouths
2. No sign whatsoever of termites, because they are hiding

If all the items on this checklist check out to your satisfaction, it's time to make the standard Insulting Opening Offer on the house, which we'll cover in our next chapter.

3

How to Get
Very Deeply into Debt

If you want to come out a winner in the negotiations for your new house, you have to
be tough. "This is not a time for human decency," are the words of Wayne Savage, the
internationally renowned lecturer and author of the best-selling book on negotiating
strategy, *Leave Them Bleeding in the Dirt*,

which retails for $178.63 and not a penny less. Which is why you need to know:

Negotiating

HOW TO NEGOTIATE LIKE A REAL SLIMEBALL

A fine example of the kind of negotiating approach you should take can be found in the excellent corporate training film *The Godfather*, where, as part of his negotiations with a movie producer, Marlon Brando gains a subtle psychological advantage by arranging to have the producer wake up in bed next to the head of a deceased horse. (It could have been worse; it could have been Marlon Brando.)

This is not to suggest that to get a good price on a house, you need to go around decapitating domesticated animals. No indeed; wild animals are more than adequate for most residential transactions. But the point is, you have to be firm.

At the outset of your negotiations, it is very important to create the impression that you don't really want to buy the house at all, that in fact you *hate* the house, and the mere *thought* of it makes you physically ill. Your opening offer should convey this. It should be worded as follows: "We don't want your house, so we will give you X number of dollars for it, including all major appliances and the children." (Note that you should *not* name a specific amount. You should actually use the term "X number of dollars," so as to avoid tipping your hand.) The broker will take your offer to the seller, who at this point has a number of options, such as:

1. He can accept your offer.
2. He can reject your offer.
3. He can give back the dinette set, the pool

table, AND the Epcot Center vacation in exchange for whatever is behind curtain number two.

Another possibility is that he will make a counteroffer, which your broker will bring back for you to consider. "We don't want to sell the house," it might say. "We only put it on the market because we enjoy having total strangers come around and test-flush all our toilets. But we are willing to let it go for Y number of dollars, plus you can have little Deirdre, provided you raise her in a religious environment. We get the microwave."

And then you send the broker back with another offer, and they send you *another* counteroffer, and so on until the broker, his fingers bloodied from typing up the various negotiating positions, drops dead in the street from exhaustion, which is the signal for the buyer and the seller to settle on a price equal to the original asking price minus about five percent. This is the price that everybody always winds up at, and if we all just agreed on it at the beginning, there would be a lot less hassle and inconvenience in the form of dead brokers. But we have to ask ourselves if this would really be such a desirable outcome.

In any event, now that you and the seller have set a price, you need to sign the agreement of sale, which should be worded in standard legal terminology, as follows:

Standard Agreement of Sale

WHEREAS the Seller wants to sell, and the Buyer wants to buy, and they think they got a price that's not too low or too high; and the Buyer gave the Seller a down payment to hold, now he'll try to get a mortgage 'fore they BOTH grow old; and the Seller's gonna see if he got termites in his place 'cause if he does, the Buyer's gonna tear it right up in his face; but if everything is cool and nobody's late, then the deal will go down on the Settlement Date.

CHORUS

Oooh baby baby
We gon' have a transaction tonight

Of course I realize you probably don't understand some of this "legal jargon," but this is only because you are stupid. This is why it's important to ask several lawyers to give you contradictory advice before you sign anything, including get-well cards.

Meanwhile, however, it is time to go around to some banks and see if you can find one foolish enough to lend you some money.

ARE YOU FINANCIALLY FIT?

The first thing you need to do is perform a detailed financial analysis of how much money you have versus how much you're going to need to buy your house. The way you do this is you draw up what professional accountants call a "Balance Sheet," which should look like this:

Money you need:

Money you have:

Money You Have

1. Savings account: $927.62

2. Checking account: Conceivably as much

as $83.15, provided that the check you wrote to Mister Muffler has not been cashed yet

3. Other assets, primarily canned goods and undeveloped photographs of the airplane wing taken during your trip to Disney World: $44.02

Money You Need to Buy a House

1. Cost to pay random lawyers for God knows what (see "The Ritual Closing Ceremony"): $6,765.90
2. Cost to have various inspectors come around and hold clipboards and shine flashlights at things but fail to notice any sign that the heating system is going to explode moments after you take possession of your new home: $1,250
3. Taxes: $3,856.90
4. Additional taxes that nobody ever mentioned to you: $4,847.89
5. Taxes that are just now being rushed into law and will apply only to your specific house purchase: $5,563.92

6. "Points," which is technically defined as "money that for some reason you have to give the bank, even though *you* are the one trying to buy the goddamn house, and no matter how many times you ask, you will never be given an intelligible explanation for this": $8,745.00

7. Other (phone deposit, cost of actual house, etc.): $126,436.06

Now, using these figures, we can create the following graphic representation to compare the amount of money you have with the amount you need:

So we can see from this financial analysis that you are definitely going to need the bank to give you a lot of money in the form of a mortgage. The bank is willing to do this because, the way mortgages are set up, no matter how many payments you make, *you still owe the bank all the money you ever borrowed*. Really. This explains why, in all your wide circle of friends, you don't know a single person who ever came close to paying off a mortgage. When you have a mortgage, at the end of every year the bank sends you a statement like this:

YOUR OUTSTANDING BALANCE AS
OF THE BEGINNING OF THE YEAR:
$93,423.54
YOUR TOTAL PAYMENTS MADE DUR-
ING THE YEAR: $11,647.32
YOUR OUTSTANDING BALANCE AS
OF THE END OF THE YEAR:
$93,423.54

It may seem as though the banks are taking unfair advantage of consumers here,
but they really have no choice. A few years
back, they lent billions and billions of dollars to the Third World, which had promised
to spend the money on factories and heavy
machinery, but which in fact lost it gambling
on rooster fights. And since the banks can't
very well march down to the Southern
Hemisphere and repossess, for example,
Brazil, you can understand why they have
no choice but to get the money from average
everyday unarmed consumers such as yourself.

All mortgages work basically the same
way: You sign a bunch of papers, then you
make large monthly payments until the Second Coming. Nevertheless, the top Con-

sumer Money Geeks all recommend that you "shop around" for your mortgage, because there are a number of different kinds available, each with its own terms, conditions, feeding habits, and so forth. Some of the more popular ones are:

- The Fixed-Rate Mortgage
- The Variable-Rate Mortgage
- The Mortgage Whose Rate Is Based on What Order the Teams Finish in the National League East
- The Mortgage with a Real Low Rate That Is Advertised in Huge Print in the Newspaper But Nobody Ever Actually Gets It
- The Balloon Mortgage
- The Party Hat Mortgage
- The Mortgage That Is Really the Expired Warranty for a 1966 Sears Washing Machine
- The Mortgage of the Living Dead

Here's an important piece of advice to bear in mind when you're shopping around for your mortgage: *Don't be intimidated.* Sure, the bank is a great big, rich, powerful financial institution and you are a small, worthless piece of scum. But that doesn't mean you should walk into the bank with your hat in your hand, like some kind of beggar! Not at all! You should *crawl* into the bank!

Ha ha! Just kidding, of course. You have nothing to worry about. All the bank will ask you to do is supply the home phone number of everybody you have ever known, even casually, since the fourth grade. Then you'll have an interview with a Loan Officer, who'll ask you a few standard screening questions, such as: "To get this mortgage, are you willing to lick the gum wads off my shoe bottoms?"

Assuming that you come up with the correct answers ("yes") to these questions, your mortgage application will be sent on to the Committee to Hold Up All the Mortgage Applications for Several Months. This will give you time to practice signing checks in preparation for the Ritual Closing Ceremony.

THE RITUAL CLOSING CEREMONY

This is an important and highly traditional part of the home-buying process, the last major hurdle you must clear before you become an Official Homeowner. It is comparable to the initiation ceremonies at major college fraternities, where, to prove that he is worthy of the privileges and responsibilities of membership, the pledge must perform some feat such as attending a Papal Mass wearing only a softball glove.

Essentially, what you must do, in the Ritual Closing Ceremony, is go into a small room and write large checks to total strangers. According to tradition, *anybody* may ask you for a check, for any amount, and you may not refuse. Once you get started handing out money, the good news will travel quickly through the real estate community via joyful shouts: "A Closing Ceremony is taking place!" Soon there will be a huge horde of people—lawyers, bankers, brokers, insurance people, termite inspectors, caterers, photographers, people you used to know in high school—crowding into the closing room and spilling out into the street. You may be forced to hurl batches of signed blank checks out the window, just to make sure that everyone is accommodated in the traditional way.

Another ritual task you must perform during the Closing Ceremony is frown with feigned comprehension at various unintelligible documents that will be placed in front of you by random individuals wearing suits:

RANDOM INDIVIDUAL: Now, as you can see, this is the Declaration of your Net Interest Accrual Payments of Debenture.

YOU (frowning): Yes.

RANDOM INDIVIDUAL: And this is the Notification of your Pro Rata Indemnities of Assumption.

YOU: Certainly.

RANDOM INDIVIDUAL: And this is the digestive system of a badger.

YOU: Of course.

Once the various officials present are satisfied that you truly wish to become a homeowner and have no checks left, they will award you a mortgage, which will spell out your new duties and obligations in standard legal terminology.

Mortgage

Hear ye, hear ye, everybody listen up because the MORTGAGOR, hereinafter referred to as the MORTGAGEE, has, by duly picking up this piece of paper and putting his JOHN HANCOCK thereontofore, committed himself and his family and his distant relatives and unborn children and domesticated animals body and soul to the terms and conditions of this MORT-

GAGE, whether these terms and conditions are actually stated right here in print on the MORTGAGE or exist only in the form of vague concepts in the minds of LAWYERS working for the BANK, to wit:

1. The money has to BE THERE on the first of the month, rain or shine.
2. If the money is not THERE, the BANK is going to get VERY ANGRY.
3. The BANK is going to want to GET EVEN.
4. The BANK is going to make SOMEBODY wish he was naked and tied down spread-eagle on an anthill with ants eating his EYEBALLS because that would be a lot more pleasant than what the BANK has in mind IF THE MONEY IS NOT THERE.
5. Specifically, the BANK is going to get a pair of NUMBER SIX KNITTING NEEDLES and heat them up to 11,000 DEGREES FAHRENHEIT, and then the BANK is going to . . .

And so it continues, in technical legalistic detail. It's really nothing to concern yourself

about. The important thing is: at last you're
a *homeowner*. Now you can immerse yourself
in the many rewarding and traditional activities that new homeowners engage in,
such as trying to figure out how to make the
mortgage payment and, simultaneously, not
starve to death.

BUDGET MEALS FOR NEW HOMEOWNERS

Dixie Cups Filled with Sugar

This easy-to-prepare meal is not only eco-
nomical, but also extremely popular with
children, who find it gives them that "extra
energy" boost they sometimes need to stay
awake for six days in a row.

Wedding Reception Food

If you go to any major hotel or country club
on a weekend, chances are you'll find a large
formal wedding reception going on, featur-

ing serving people walking around and actually *giving away* teeny little sandwiches with the crust cut off. This is an excellent source of food for you, the new homeowner. You just walk in there, looking like you are a close personal friend of either the bride or the groom, and help yourself to as many trays as you feel you will need during this particular mortgage payment period. To keep people from getting suspicious, you should stop from time to time and remark aloud, in a natural tone of voice: "I am a close personal friend of the bride! Or the groom!"

This technique also works at funeral receptions ("I am very sorry that the deceased is dead!").

But enough about food. Because before we can worry about paying for our house, we have to move into it and start finding out what's wrong with it. My guess is, plenty.

4

Moving:
A Common Mistake

I, personally, have never given birth to a child, but I have seen it dramatized a number of times on television, and I would say that in terms of pain, childbirth does not hold a candle to moving. For one thing, childbirth has a definite end to it. The baby comes out, looking like a vaseline-smeared ferret, and the parents get to beam at it joy-

Moving—
a common mistake

fully, and that is that. Whereas the average move goes on forever. You take Couple A, who just had a baby, and Couple B, who just moved their household, and if you keep track of them, you'll find that years from now, when Couple A's baby has grown up, left home, and started a family, Couple B will still be rooting through boxes full of wadded-up newspaper, looking for the lid to their Mr. Coffee. Also, during childbirth, when things go wrong, trained professionals give you powerful drugs. Nobody is ever this thoughtful during a move.

This is why my Number One piece of helpful advice to people who are about to move, especially for the first time, is always:

DON'T DO IT! SET FIRE TO YOUR HOUSEHOLD GOODS RIGHT NOW AND JUST WALK AWAY FROM THEM WITHOUT SO MUCH AS A BACKWARD GLANCE! THIS WILL BE EASIER, IN THE LONG RUN!

Of course you think I'm just kidding, and by the time you realize I'm not, you'll already be in your new home, trying unsuccessfully to locate something to slash your wrists with. So we might as well get started.

First off, you need to make an important decision: Are you going to move yourself with the help of friends who have been drinking too much beer, or are you going to hire surly, incompetent professionals? The answer most likely depends on whether or not you, personally, have to pay for it. Many times, large corporations will pay for moving expenses, so you might ask them, although usually their policy is to do this only for their own employees.

PROFESSIONAL MOVERS: HOW TO GET YOUR POSSESSIONS BACK

The big advantage of going with professional movers, of course, is that you have somebody to complain to when you get to your new home and discover that your fine china has been reduced to Chiclet-size pieces and there is mayonnaise in the piano. Also, if it's a full-service move, you get to watch the Packing People in action. These are moving company workers who go through your house scooping up everything they see and putting it into a box. *Everything*. The Packing People do not ask questions. They will cheerfully pack an entire box with used Kitty Litter, painstakingly wrapping each individual cat doot in specialized paper so it will not be damaged in shipment. Thus it is very important to keep a sharp eye on the Packing People while they are at work, so as

The Pros:

to avoid painful tragedies. ("WHAT HAVE YOU DONE WITH JENNIFER?")

Another problem that sometimes arises with professional movers is getting them to give you your furniture back once they put it

in the van. This problem is especially serious if the driver, after he puts your stuff in
his van, goes around and picks up several
other households full of stuff, which he then
has to drop off, usually in Zaire, before he
can go to your new home. The solution to
this problem is to do what savvy moving
families have been doing for years: *hijack
the truck*. Get a gun, and simply demand
that the driver unload at your house first. Of
course this means you'll wind up with somebody else's possessions, but it doesn't really
matter. You'll never get them unpacked anyway.

MOVING YOURSELF

The big advantage of moving yourself is that
you get to rent a rental truck. Rental trucks
are highly specialized vehicles that are not re-
leased for use by the general public until they
have undergone an intensive "breaking-in"
program of being used to carry violent cattle
with severe intestinal disorders over rough

The Rental Truck

terrain for a minimum of 1,700,000 miles without maintenance.

These machines are capable of traveling the length of several football fields on a single tankful of gas, yet they boast the kind of cornering, braking, and acceleration characteristics normally associated with municipal stadiums. No question about it: Once you get behind the wheel of a rental truck, you'll wonder what the sticky substance on the seat is. But before you're ready to think about the truck, you need to go through all your possessions and make a serious futile effort to get rid of them. A key element in this effort is . . .

THE GARAGE SALE

A garage sale is basically when strangers come to your house and examine your personal belongings with undisguised contempt.

The first ones you'll meet will be the garage sale Regulars. Garage sales are their lives. They'll show up at your home early, generally about two days before the sale is scheduled to begin. The way they find out about it is, they use computers to examine satellite reconnaissance photographs of suburban neighborhoods for signs of incipient garage sale activity, such as people standing around arguing about how much to charge for a 1953 set of the *Encyclo-*

The Garage Sale

pedia Britannica that's missing volume 18 (Saliva-Tapeworm).

How do you price all those treasured personal belongings? The truth is, it doesn't matter what you charge, because the Regulars aren't going to pay it. These are people who do not own a single possession, including furniture, that they paid more than $2.50 for, and they are not about to change their policy for the likes of *you*.

GARAGE SALE REGULAR (picking up a sale object): What's this?

YOU: That's my grandmother's brooch. It's

twenty-four-carat gold, it has eight flawless diamonds, and these are real pearls in the center here. It was presented to my grandmother personally by the King of England, whose crest is on the back.

GARAGE SALE REGULAR: I'll give you a dollar for it.

The Regulars will quickly pick you clean of everything that anybody might want to buy, so when your sale actually gets under way, it will consist of people getting out of their cars, examining your possessions the way you might view an unexpected leech in your pasta, then asking you: "Is this *it*?" The only thing they'll be interested in buying is anything on which you have carefully placed a large sign stating: NOT FOR SALE. They'll walk up, read the sign carefully, then ask you: "Is this for sale?"

It can make you feel vaguely inadequate, watching people reject your possessions. At least that's how it affects me. I find myself wanting to *please* these people. I want to say, "If you don't see what you like, we'll order it!" But of course this tends to defeat the whole purpose of the garage sale, so the best thing to do is just sit there grimly until the sale is over and you can throw everything away.

Okay, now that we've cleared out some of the dead wood, it's time to proceed with the next step in the moving process, which is . . .

GETTING A BUNCH OF EMPTY LIQUOR BOXES AND HURLING THINGS INTO THEM AT RANDOM

You won't start out this way, of course. You'll start by selecting the objects with great care and wrapping them up very gently. You'll keep this up for a week or so, packing box after box, making regular trips for more, getting to be good buddies with the clerks at the liquor store, getting a satisfied feeling when you gaze upon the big stacks of filled boxes in the living room. And then one day you'll look around and make a chilling discovery: *You're not making any progress.* There's still just as much stuff lying around unboxed as there was the day you started.

There might even be *more*. And so you start to pack with less care, faster and faster, until you find yourself in an uncontrolled packing frenzy, throwing everything—dirt, money, deceased spiders—into liquor boxes in a desperate effort to empty the house.

It's impossible to empty a house.

What you are up against here is a strange phenomenon that has astounded scientists and liquor store clerks for thousands of years: *It is impossible to empty a house.* You can't do it. Somehow, word that you're moving gets out to all the dumps and garbage disposal sites, and in the dead of the night there comes an eerie rustling sound as all your old possessions, the ones you threw away years ago—broken appliances, coffee grounds, Pat Boone records—rise up and come limping and scuttling back to your house, where they nestle in the backs of your closets, waiting to spring out at you the way Tony Perkins kept springing out at people in *Psycho*, only more unexpectedly. If you throw them away again, they'll crawl right back the next night. Eventually you'll lose your sanity, and you'll start deciding to keep them. "This looks like it's in pretty good shape!" you'll say, holding up the owner's manual to the Chevrolet station wagon that you sold in 1972. And all the other old possessions, back in their closets, writhe with joy, because they know there is hope for them.

This is how deranged you can become: The last time we moved, I had to physically restrain my wife from packing several scum-encrusted rags that I had been using to clean toilets. It was also my wife who decided to keep the greenish chair that looks like what would happen if a monstrous prehistoric creature blew its nose in our living room. We had remarked many times before that all the pain and anguish of moving would be justified by the fact that we would be leaving this chair behind forever. It broke into open laughter when it was carried into our new home.

HELPFUL PACKING HINTS:

- After packing a box, always write your name on the top (e.g., "Barry"), so when you get to your new home you'll be able to tell at a glance what your name is.
- Tropical fish should be individually wadded up in newspaper.
- In fact, it's a good idea to pack several boxes full of nothing *but* wadded-up pieces of newspaper, so you'll have plenty on hand in your New Home.
- When packing perishable items, such as yogurt, make a mental note to throw them away immediately upon arrival in your new home.
- Be sure to take along at least 2,800 pounds of your old college textbooks with titles like *Really Long Poems of the Six-*

teenth Century, the ones you never read when you were in college, the ones that are still packed in boxes from four moves ago. These are sure to come in handy.

- It is best not to pack important prescription drugs such as tranquilizers. It is best to keep them on hand and gulp them down like salted peanuts.

Another total breakdown of rational thought occurs when you start deciding to leave behind things, as little gifts, for the new owners. You will look at your collection of seventeen thousand cans of various paints, none of which has been opened since the Protestant Reformation and each of which contains about a quarter inch of sludge hardened to the consistency of dental porcelain, and you will say: "The new owners will probably be able to use these!" You will say the same thing about the swing set gradually oxidizing into a major rust formation in the backyard, even though you know the new owners are a childless couple in their seventies. You will leave them your old eyeglasses, deceased radios, filthy rags, and baked goods supporting fourth-generation mold colonies. You will leave them half-filled bags of lawn chemicals that have, over the decades, become bonded permanently to the garage floor. Near the end, you will display not the slightest shred of human decency:

YOU (brightly): I'm sure the new owners would like to have *this*!

YOUR SPOUSE: That's your *mother*!

HOW TO MOVE A PET

My major experience with moving a pet was the time we moved our dog, Earnest, from Pennsylvania to Florida via airplane. We took her to these professional pet transporters, who told us that for $357.12, which is approximately $357.12 more than we originally paid for Earnest, they would put her on the airplane in a special cage, which we would get to keep. The reason for this generosity became clear when I picked Earnest up at the Miami airport. It had been a long flight, and since Earnest had had nothing to read, she had passed the time by pooping, so you can imagine what the inside of her cage looked and smelled like, on top of which, as soon as she saw me, she went into the classic Dance of Lunatic Unrestrained Dog Joy Upon Sighting the Master, yelping and whirling like the agitator on an unbalanced washing machine, creating a veritable poop tornado inside the cage, just dying to get out and say hi.

In fact, this experience gave me an idea for a powerful and semihumane global strategic weapon, which would be called "The

Moving a pet

Earnest." The way it would work is, we'd get some large and friendly dogs, such as Labrador retrievers, and we'd keep them in cages for maybe a week, feeding them bulky foods, then we'd parachute them into the Soviet Union. The cages would open automatically on impact with the ground, and these lonely and highly aromatic dogs would come bounding out, desperate to lavish affection all over the human race, and that would be the end of Soviet civilization as we now know it. Of course there is always the danger of escalation. The Russians might come back at us with, for example, St. Bernards. Maybe we'd better just forget it.

Another way to move your pet, of course, is to take it with you in the car. The problem here is that most motels don't allow animals. I know of one couple who once got a dog into a motel by claiming it was a Seeing Eye dog, which they established via the clever ruse of having the husband wear dark glasses, only the dog didn't really hold up its end of the bargain. Instead of acting like a trained professional, being alert, looking out for obstacles, and so forth, it was dragging its owner along like a motorboat towing a reluctant water-skier, stopping only to sniff people's crotches and snork up low-lying cocktail peanuts. Another problem with the Seeing Eye ruse is that it won't work if your pet is a snake, for example, or a cat. There *are* no Seeing Eye cats, of course, because the sole function of cats, in the Great Chain of Life, is to cause harm to human beings.

The instant a cat figured out that the blind person would follow it wherever it went, it would lead this person directly into whirling unshielded manufacturing equipment.

I once, as a favor to my sister, transported her cat in my car about ninety miles to her new apartment. Naturally it turned out that the only place in the entire car that the cat wanted to be was *directly under the brake pedal*, which meant that if I needed to slow down, I had to reach down there and grab the cat without looking—an activity comparable to groping around for a moray eel in a dark underwater cave filled with barbed wire—and then I'd hurl the cat, still clinging to pieces of my flesh, into the backseat, and then I'd hit the brakes, and then the cat would scuttle back under the pedal. As you can imagine, this cat and I were the best of friends by the time we arrived at my sister's apartment, and I only hope that I see it again someday when my hand has healed to the point where I can aim a dart gun.

HOW TO MOVE CHILDREN

Children are more difficult to move than pets. You can't just put a child in a crate and stick him on an airplane. God knows I have tried.

The important thing is preparation. Psychologists stress that you should break the news of the move to the child as soon as possible, ideally at birth. "We're going to move!" you should shout gaily, the instant the child's head emerges from the mother. The child will probably cry at this news, but this is normal. Most children are unhappy about moving, which is why it is so important, at each stage in the move preparation process, to sit down with them, one on one, and lie to them.

"It's going to be *such* fun!" you should tell them. "You're going to make *lots* of new friends!"

Of course this is probably not true. Probably they will wind up in a school where all the really good social cliques have already reached their full membership quotas and have long waiting lists. Probably your children will immediately be branded with life-

long unflattering nicknames such as Goat Booger. But there is no point in telling them this now.

A SMART MOVING IDEA FOR TWO-CAR FAMILIES

If you're moving a long distance, you're probably wondering what's the best way to get both cars to your new home. One way, of course, is for the wife to drive one car and the husband to drive the other, but this can be lonely and tiring, especially if there are small children, who will of course be clawing foot-long strips of each other's flesh off before you have pulled out of the driveway. So what modern moving professionals recommend is that you *let the children drive one of the cars.* This way, the adults, in Car A, can relax and talk or listen to classical music, while the children, in Car B, can amuse themselves by playing imaginative highway games such as Death Avengers of the Interstate, and you can all arrive at the motel in a good mood, ready to enjoy a relaxed and

happy evening together until the police
come.

MOVING YOUR POSSESSIONS
INTO YOUR NEW HOME

If you are moving yourself, you simply wait
for the most humid day in the history of the
world, pull your truck up outside your new
home, and start carrying your possessions
inside. Every hour or so you should take a
break, which will give your possessions an
opportunity to scurry, giggling, back out to
the truck, so that you may carry them inside
again.

If you are using professional movers, the
correct procedure is as follows:

1. You stand in the middle of the living
   room.
2. Hundreds of burly, impatient, sweating
   moving company men come swarming at
   you from all directions carrying identical
   brown cardboard boxes, each of which

has your last name written on it in a helpful manner.

3. "WHERE DO YOU WANT THIS?" say the burly, impatient men, making it clear by their tone of voice that if you do not answer them within *two seconds*, they will sweat so hard that they warp your floor.

4. You pick a room at random. "That goes in the spare bedroom," you say. Or: "In the dining room, please." It makes no difference. They will put it wherever they want. Sometimes, for fun, the movers will completely fill up a room, floor to ceiling, with boxes, thus creating a humongous Rubik's Cube out of your worldly goods, so that to get to any one box, you have to move 1,357 others in exactly the right pattern. I warned you, way back at the beginning of this chapter, that it would be easier to just set fire to everything, but of course you wouldn't listen.

UNPACKING

It is best not to attempt this all at once. It is best to space it out over a period of several years, so that you may savor the joy of discovering the kinds of comical items you chose to pack and, at great cost in money and effort, move to your new home. You can even make this a traditional nightly family event, with everybody gathering around a packing box and laughing festively as you unwrap 750 square feet of protective wrapping paper to discover, say, the key that operates the radiator of your former home.

WHAT CONDITION THE PREVIOUS OWNERS WILL HAVE LEFT YOUR NEW HOME IN

They will have left it in roughly the same condition as the Visigoths left Rome in. When you open the refrigerator, life-threatening molds will try to grasp you with their tentacles. But do not judge the previous owners too harshly; remember that when they left, they were in the same subhuman, totally amoral moving-induced state of mind that *you* were in when you moved out of your house without so much as a backward glance at the inch-thick layer of crud that got baked onto the sides of your former oven when the lasagna exploded.

GETTING YOUR NEW PHONE, GAS, ELECTRICITY, APPLIANCES, CABLE TELEVISION, AND WATER HOOKED UP

The important thing to understand is that *all these things are done by the same person*. Yes, homeowners: there is only one Hookup Man in the *entire world*, sort of like Santa Claus, and as you can imagine, he is very, very busy. This is why, when you call up the telephone company to find out when the Hookup Man will visit your house, they cannot pinpoint the exact time. "Right now," they will say, "it looks like it will probably be an even-numbered year." In fact most people have never seen the Hookup Man, and some say he is only a legend. But many of us believe in him, because we have seen the jolly pranks and tricks he likes to play, our favorite being the one where we have been waiting for him in our house for days, and finally we must go out for food, and the instant we are gone he comes bounding out of the bushes, where he has been hiding, and leaves a cheerful note on our door that says: "Sorry We Missed You!" Ha ha! Such a card, that Hookup Man!

5

Making New Enemies

Probably the most important thing, in settling into a new home, is to establish good relationships with your neighbors. The reason for this is best summarized by the moving words of the famous English poet John Donne, who wrote:

No man is an island unto his own personal self;

Each man is more of a subcontinent,
So never send to ask for whom the doorbell
tolls
Because more than likely it is your neigh-
bor
Come to see if you have a plumber's snake
he can borrow
So he can attempt to unclog the hall toilet
Which he suspects his son has flushed
His daughter's Rainbow Brite doll down.

Idealistic? Sure it is, but it still has meaning today. We live in a complex, intercon-
nected society, and sometimes we must call
upon our neighbors to help us, to stand by
us, to comfort us, or at very least to try not
to back their recreational vehicle into our
Jacuzzi. So as soon as you get to your new
home, you want to Reach Out. You want to
march right next door, put on your very nic-
est smile, ring the doorbell, and . . .

BARK BARK BARK BARK BARK BARK
Well! It looks as though your new neighbors have a doggy! A very *alert* doggy! A
doggy with jaws the size of an important ge-
ological formation! In the background, you

dimly perceive shapes that might be your new neighbors.

"Hi!" you say. "We're your new—"

BARK BARK BARK BARK BARK BARK BARK BARK BARK BARK BARK BARK BARK BARK BARK BARK BARK BARK

"BE QUIET, LAMONT!!" say your new neighbors. It sounds like there might be several of them.

"Anyway," you say, "we thought we'd stop by and—"

BARK BARK BARK BARK BARK BARK BARK BARK BARK BARK BARK BARK BARK BARK BARK BARK BARK BARK BARK BARK BARK BARK BARK BARK BARK BARK BARK BARK BARK BARK BARK BARK BARK BARK BARK BARK

"DAMMIT, LAMONT!!" say your new neighbors.

"Well, okay!" you say. "Guess we'd better get back and—"

BARK BARK BARK BARK BARK BARK BARK BARK BARK BARK BARK BARK BARK BARK BARK BARK BARK BARK BARK BARK BARK BARK BARK BARK BARK BARK BARK BARK BARK BARK BARK BARK BARK BARK BARK BARK BARK BARK BARK BARK BARK BARK BARK BARK BARK BARK BARK BARK BARK BARK BARK BARK BARK BARK BARK BARK BARK BARK BARK BARK BARK BARK BARK BARK BARK BARK BARK BARK BARK BARK BARK BARK

BARK BARK BARK BARK BARK BARK BARK BARK

They seem like nice people.

Now that you've met the neighbors, it's time to start locating some of the "necessities of life." If you have small children, you need to find a Pediatric Group where you can go and sit in the waiting room when your children get their ears infected, which is approximately four times per child per week.

Notice I say "Pediatric Group," not "Pediatrician." There are no longer any Lone Ranger–style pediatricians, because it is considered a serious violation of modern medical ethics for a child to see the same doctor twice during the child's lifetime. This is why you sometimes must wait so long in the waiting room: The Pediatric Group is flying in a new doctor, sometimes from as far away as Malaysia, solely to avoid having your child see a familiar face. This is also why, in selecting a new Pediatric Group, the most important factor is not the doctors, but *the person who answers the phone*, because you will spend a large portion of your life talking with this person:

Choosing a pediatric group

PHONE PERSON: Good afternoon, this is Pediatricians Backwards "R" Us; how may we help you?

YOU: Hi, this is Mrs. Evans, and my son, Thad, has been having these kind of strange-shaped bowel movements, and last time this happened we saw Dr. Wexler, and he said if it happened again we should call and—

PHONE PERSON: Well, of course you realize you can't see Dr. Wexler ever again.

YOU: Yes, of course, but I was wondering if maybe Dr. Bunderson—

PHONE PERSON (suspiciously): How do you know Dr. Bunderson? Have you seen him before?

YOU (quickly): No! No! Really! I just *heard* of him, that's all. From a friend.

PHONE PERSON: Well, in that case, please hold.

*** eighteen-minute pause ***

PHONE PERSON: Dr. Bunderson wants to know what you mean by "strange-shaped."

YOU: Well, kind of like M & M's.

PHONE PERSON: Please hold.

*** twenty-three-minute pause ***

PHONE PERSON: Plain or peanut?

YOU: Plain. Shall I hold?

PHONE PERSON: Of course.

*** Forty-nine-minute pause ***

PHONE PERSON: Dr. Bunderson wants you to bring Thad in and sit in the waiting room for two hours reading books with names like *Billy the Bunny Bumps His Nose* and listening to children shriek behind closed doors, after which Dr. Bunderson will see you for slightly under a minute and a half and prescribe a medicine that you have to administer anally when your child is sleeping and that costs as much per ounce as a round-trip Concorde ticket to Paris, France.

YOU (gratefully): Thank you.

Important as it is to find a Pediatric Group, it is not the *most* important task, because it is merely a matter of life and death, which means it pales by comparison with the task of:

FINDING SOMEBODY TO FIX YOUR CAR

This has become very difficult in recent years, because most gas stations have switched over to being "convenience" stores, meaning that, in addition to gas, they sell food such as bologna sandwiches

created right around the time of the Big
Bang. But they do not fix cars. You pull
into a modern gas station with an actual
car problem, and odds are that the cashier,
sitting behind the bulletproof glass watching MTV, will have the police come and arrest you for blocking the access of
legitimate customers wishing to purchase
Slim Jims, cheap sunglasses, and Tic-Tac
breath mints.

The reason gas stations sell food, of
course, is that the supermarkets are busy
cashing checks. The supermarkets have to
cash checks because the banks are busy
mailing unsolicited credit cards to everybody
in the Western Hemisphere. The result is
that very few people fix cars.

The best way to select a new mechanic is
to conduct a little competence test, wherein
you deliberately disconnect one spark plug
wire from your car's engine. Then you go
around to various gas stations, tell the at-
tendants that you think something is wrong
with your engine, and see if they can cor-
rectly diagnose the problem.

INCORRECT DIAGNOSIS: "So?"

CORRECT DIAGNOSIS: "Sounds like

something is wrong with your, whaddyacall-it, engine."

If you find somebody who gives you the correct diagnosis, you should cling to him the way the remora clings to the shark. If you have a daughter, you should encourage her to marry him.

SELECTING A SUPERMARKET

The major things we look for in a supermarket are:

1. A wide selection of browsing material at the checkout counter in the form of *People* magazine and tabloid-size newspapers with headlines like "BURT REYNOLDS WEDS GIANT UFO CENTIPEDE"
2. A policy whereby people who get in the checkout line clutching large, time-consuming wads of food coupons are actually charged *more* for their groceries.
3. *Very* strict enforcement of the ten-item limit in the express lane. Ideally, this en-

forcement would involve a trapdoor. ("Oh? Do I have fourteen items? I didn't realIIIEEEEEEEEEEEEEE . . .")

JOINING LOCAL CLUBS AND ORGANIZATIONS

This is an excellent way for a newcomer like yourself to make friends with many local community leaders, all of whom will want to sell you insurance.

GIVING MONEY TO THE LOCAL POLICE BENEVOLENT ASSOCIATION

We always do this. Whenever they come around, we give them a generous contribution and a cheerful smile, because deep in our souls we have this nagging fear that they write your name down somewhere, and if you did *not* contribute, it will come back to haunt you:

YOU: Help! Please send somebody to 465 Magnolia Street immediately!

POLICE DISPATCHER: Would that be the residence of Stanley Johnson, the guy who stiffed the Benevolent Association for six straight years? The guy who always says he'll send us a check "next week"?

YOU: Yes! Please! A huge insane man is pounding on our door with an axe!

POLICE DISPATCHER: That would be Lester Stubbins. Last year he donated, let's see here, twenty-five dollars.

YOU: HE'S BREAKING DOWN THE DOOR! HURRY!!

POLICE DISPATCHER: Sure thing. We'll have a unit there "next week".

SELECTING A SCHOOL FOR YOUR CHILD

There are two major kinds of schools:

Public Schools, defined as "schools where the doors have been removed from the bathroom stalls."

Private Schools, defined as "schools you cannot afford."

The key factor in selecting a school, of course, is what kind of nurse it has. Remember that the primary function of the American educational system is to provide you with a place to leave your children when you go to work; if the school has the kind of nurse who calls you up every time some little thing goes wrong, the whole point is defeated. Also, your career could be ruined:

SETTING:
The chambers of the U.S. Supreme Court
YOU: In conclusion, your honors, I wish to state that my client—
CHIEF JUSTICE (interrupting): Counsel, I have a note here from the nurse at the Bob-o-Link Elementary School stating that your daughter, Jennifer, is throwing up what appears to be Yoo-Hoo brand chocolate drink.

So you're looking for a school with a level-headed nurse, the kind who would not *think* of calling you over something as minor as vomiting, which most small children engage in purely as a recreational activity.

Another thing: Whichever school you select, *you must get your child into the "gifted" class*. I imagine there was a time when the word "gifted" was used to describe only children who were above average, but since hardly any parents today will tolerate the thought that their child may be average, the term "gifted" is now applied to any student with more brain wave activity than a glazed doughnut.

The way you get your child into the gifted class is, you go to the school personally and make it clear to the staff that you are a Concerned Parent, meaning a potentially humongous pain in the ass. You should demand to see the curriculum, so as to make sure that, at each grade level, your child will receive instruction in the subjects appropriate for a standard American education, namely:

GRADE	SUBJECTS LEARNED
K-2	Not to cross the street; not to take drugs; not to get in strange cars; not to talk to

people; not to trust anybody;
the Pledge of Allegiance

3-7   How to make science fair projects proving that ice is actually frozen water; the state
capitals; designer jeans

8-12   Sex

Of course you need not worry too much
about your child's progress, because the
school will keep you posted by means of report cards, which in most schools are now
completely computerized to guard against
the danger that anybody might be able to
understand them. Our son's report card
looks like this:

AmStudSocBio   67 87 1123.43
                    54.45%
PhysLangMath   1223.44343 4-4
                    ******

SocMathStudAm-   2948-
BioPhys   09849238409
Cincinnati   001 020 004
East   Pass
   →NOTE: Your Mileage May Vary←

When we get our son's report card, we make a big show of examining it with concerned frowns identical to the ones we use when our mechanic shows us broken pieces of our car, but the truth is we have no idea how well our son is doing.

ENROLLING YOUR CHILDREN IN SEVERAL DOZEN AFTER-SCHOOL ACTIVITIES

Believe it or not, there was once a time when parents did not enroll their children in after-school activities. In those primitive times, when children came home from school, they'd just go outside, completely on their own, and engage in what professional child psychologists call "nonstructured" behavior, also known as "playing," which is when you

- run around shrieking and getting dirt in your hair
- hold elaborate funerals for stuffed animals
- lie on your back next to a friend and make

94

burping noises until one of you laughs so
hard that he pees in his pants
• pretend you are fighting evil aliens from
the Planet Kawoomba, who can be defeated only by spit

And so on. Of course, today we realize
that children need to have a great deal of
structure in the form of leagues and uni-
forms and referees and team photographs
and trophies and dozens of parents standing
on the sidelines shrieking like mental pa-
tients. So unless you are some kind of low-
life child-abusing vermin, one of the first
things you'll do when you move to your new
home is enroll your children in Little
League, soccer, and midget football, as well
as a scouting program, not to mention gym-
nastics, ballet, violin, karate, computer, ten-
nis, and helicopter-piloting lessons. You
want your child's life to become so struc-
tured that he or she is incapable of fooling
around in his or her own yard without detailed instructions from a coach. ("OK, Ja-
son! Burp! NO, dammit! Not that way!")

Not that we have time to worry about our
child's education or after-school activities.

No, we are busy working and striving, in hopes that someday we will be able to afford something that most Americans dream of but very few ever achieve: nice furniture. We'll cover this depressing topic in a later chapter. But first we need to look, in the next chapter, at the basic condition of our house, and see if we can't, by means of various costly projects, make it worse.

6

It's Noon: Do You Know Where Your Contractor Is?

You may have noticed that nowhere in this book do I ever talk about how to Do It Yourself. This is because I have done a great many things myself over the years, and in every case I have ultimately come to realize that I would have been better off if I had just walked around my house firing random shotgun blasts. No matter how hard I tried, my homeowner projects always produced highly comical results, such as the enormous concrete lump in the yard of the house we owned in Pennsylvania.

I am not making this lump up. We acquired it as a result of the project when I erected a basketball post, which I needed because, as a professional writer, I often had to go outside and gain artistic inspiration by pretending I was the U.S. Olympic basketball team, challenging the Soviet team for the gold medal. The part of the Soviet team was played by my dog. You will be pleased to learn that the U.S. team always won, because (a) the Soviet team couldn't dribble— it would just sort of nose the ball around the court—and (b) the U.S. team had this very effective play where it would yell, in a stern voice: "No! BAD dog!!" which caused the Soviet team to crouch down on the court in a guilty fashion, and the United States would cruise past for an easy layup.

Anyway, the way I erected the basketball post was, carefully following the instructions that came with it, I dug a hole three feet deep and thirty inches wide. The instructions said I was supposed to put the post in the hole and fill it with concrete, only I had no concrete. I had never, until that moment, given much thought as to where concrete even *came* from. Large oceangoing freighters was my best guess.

So I looked in the yellow pages, and lo and behold, there was this place that sold concrete in special trailers that attached to your car. I called them up, and they told me each trailer held a "yard" of concrete.

"A 'yard'?" I said.

"Yes," they confirmed. "A yard." Whatever the hell that meant.

Well. It turns out that they use the name "yard" because this is enough concrete to cover North America to a depth of three feet. I had a very adventurous drive home from the concrete place, propelled by a trailer that weighed far more than my actual car, a trailer with no respect whatsoever for the tradition of stopping at red lights. But finally I made it, and I positioned the trailer over my basketball hole, and I opened the little gate at the bottom, and in one second the hole was full of concrete, using maybe one trillionth of the available supply, which I needed to find a use for pronto, because the burly men back at the concrete place had made it clear that if you bring them back a trailer full of hardened concrete, their policy is to roll it back and forth over your body.

This is when I came up with the idea of making a lump. I backed the trailer over to a section of our yard that had always looked like it could use some perking up, landscapingwise, and I created this free-form pile of concrete that is not only attractive, but also very durable. If, millions of years from now, when all other man-made structures have disappeared, intelligent life forms from other galaxies visit the planet Earth, they will find this lump, and they will wonder what kind of being created it, and for what purpose. I bet basketball will never occur to them.

And the hell of it is, the concrete lump was one of my *better* projects, in the sense that I also got a working basketball post out of it. Most of the other ones turned out much worse. The full impact of this was driven home to me forcibly when we decided to sell the Pennsylvania house, and we paid several thousand dollars (I am still not making

Do-it-yourself concrete lump

this up) to two men, both named Jonathan, to come over and eliminate all traces of all my homeowner projects—bookshelves where you could see the shapes of dead insects under the paint, paneling that looked like it had been installed by vandals, etc.—in an effort to make our home look as nice as it did before I started improving it. After the Jonathans took out all my projects, the house mostly consisted of holes, which they filled up with Spackle. When prospective buyers would ask: "What kind of construction is this house?" I would answer: "Spackle."

So to get back to my original point, I am now violently opposed to doing anything myself. I think there should be a federal law requiring people who publish do-it-yourself

books to include a warning, similar to what the Surgeon General has on cigarette packs, right on the cover of the book, stating:

WARNING: ANY MONEY YOU SAVE BY DOING HOMEOWNER PROJECTS YOURSELF WILL BE OFFSET BY THE COST OF HIRING COMPETENT PROFESSIONALS TO COME AND REMOVE THEM SO YOU CAN SELL YOUR HOUSE, NOT TO MENTION THE EMOTIONAL TRAUMA ASSOCIATED WITH LISTENING TO THESE PROFESSIONALS, AS THEY RIP OUT LARGE HUNKS OF

A PROJECT, LAUGH AND YELL REMARKS SUCH AS: "HEY! GET A LOAD OF *THIS*."

So now you are asking yourself: "Okay, if I'm not supposed to do anything myself, how am I supposed to get my house fixed?" The answer is: contractors. A contractor is a man with a pickup truck and a set of business cards that say something like:

ED BROGAN Inc.
General Contractor
All Types of Construction and Repair
30 Years Experience—Quality Work
Fully Bonded and Insured
Free Estimates—Reasonable Rates
"We Never Show Up"

No, I am of course kidding about that last line. They won't *tell* you that they never show up; this is a secret that they are sworn to uphold during the graduation ceremony at the Contractor Academy, where each man receives his Official Contractor's battered toolbox, which contains, not tools, but thousands and thousands of traditional handcrafted contractor excuses for not showing up, such as:

- "I strained my back."
- "My truck has a flat tire."
- "My wife is having a baby."
- "My uncle died."
- "My wife strained her back."
- "My uncle has a flat tire."
- "My truck is having a baby."

These time-honored excuses have been handed down through many contractor generations, dating all the way back to ancient Rome, where the original contractors built the ruins. Contrary to what historians will try to tell you, the ruins were never finished buildings: they were *always* ruins. The Romans kept trying to get the contractors to come back and finish them, but the contractors kept coming up with excuses, the oldest recorded one being "Quid vox probenium est" ("My wife strained her uncle"). Eventually the Romans simply had to learn to live among ruins. You, as a homeowner, will have to do the same thing.

THE BASIC CONTRACTING PROCESS

1. The contractor comes to your house and strides around in a confidence-inducing fashion, taking measurements and writing things down on a clipboard. What he is writing down is the batting averages of the 1978 Boston Red Sox, which he will multiply by the relative humidity to come up with an "estimate," which is legally defined as "the amount of money you will ultimately spend on phone calls in a fruitless effort to locate the contractor." Once you have agreed to the "estimate," the contractor will leave, telling you that he will come back and start work on "Thursday."

2. Four to thirteen weeks later, the contractor shows up with two workmen selected on the basis of owning T-shirts festooned with photographs of rock bands with names like "Death Penis." The contractor leaves the workmen behind and informs you that he will be back on "Thursday." Then he disappears.

3. The workmen take all of your furniture and put it out on your patio, then they

knock down a wall. Neither of these steps necessarily has anything to do with the job at hand. This is just basic contracting procedure. Having completed these tasks, the workmen take a well-earned "lunch break." They will never come back again. There is nothing you can do about this. You can search all the way through the United States Constitution, and you will find a great number of statements in there about unimportant issues such as the vice president, but you will find nothing about getting workmen back to your house. What we need is a constitutional amendment. It would say:

ARTICLE MXLICBM: If workmen come to your house and screw everything up, they shall either (a) have to come back and at least try to make it normal again or (b) be subjected to powerful electric shocks in their private parts.

Interesting Sidelight:

Modern science has been unable to determine where workmen disappear to. At one time it was believed that they went to other jobs, but we now know that there are no "other jobs," because if there were, then eventually, somewhere, some homeowner's house would actually get worked on, and you would read about this astounding event in *The New York Times*.

WORKMEN WORK ON HOME, the headline would say, and huge crowds of worshipful homeowners would flock to marvel at the worked-upon home, similar to the way the religious faithful sometimes flock to rural communities when somebody has discovered a bale of peat moss shaped like the Lord.

4. Approximately six weeks later, the contractor returns and notes with displeasure that the workmen have failed to disconnect the plumbing and electrical systems. "Always disconnect the plumbing and electrical systems, even if you are merely building an outdoor deck!" is a rule that is stressed repeatedly at the Contractor Academy. Angrily, the contractor performs these vital tasks, then, assuring you that he will be back "Thurs-

day," he disappears. You cannot grab him. A skilled contractor can actually cause himself to *dematerialize*, into hyperspace, right before your eyes.

What ultimately may happen is, you'll get so desperate that, despite my stern warnings, you will attempt to actually do things yourself. One Saturday morning you'll get up bright and early, and you'll go down to the Homeowner Hell. This is a nationwide chain of stores, each of which is approximately the size of Indonesia and is filled with billions and billions of random and obscure hardware objects such as "toggle bolts," which are packed inside special plastic blister packs, which you cannot open except with special razor knives sold only inside blister packs at Homeowner Hell. It is a comical sight indeed to see hundreds of homeowners peering at these objects with a total lack of comprehension, like fish examining a nuclear submarine. The contractors love to watch this via closed-circuit television from the Parallel Contractor Universe. It is their favorite show.

7

Redecorating for Under 650,000 Dollars

The best way to get decorating ideas is to buy several glossy interior design publications such as *Architectural Digest* ("The International Magazine of Homes Much Nicer Than Yours") and cull through the articles to obtain useful tips. The main tip you will pick up is that if you want your house to look really nice, you do not necessarily have

to have professional training or even a special "flair" for design; all you need is more money than the human mind can comprehend. You will learn this from eight-page color photo spreads featuring homes the size of Baltimore—always called "villas"—situated on dramatic mountainside real estate accessible to ordinary citizens such as yourself only by telescope. The accompanying articles sound like this:

The owners—he, a prominent industrialist neurosurgeon and president of four major investment firms: she, a bestselling novelist and Queen of Belgium—knew exactly what they wanted when they decided to build the Villa de Mucho Simoleons. "We wanted," they said, in unison, "the kind of informal and inviting home where we could entertain our friends and, if we felt like it, play polo in the foyer." Their design consultants, Wilmington A. "Bill" Sashweight IV and Marjory "Pookie" Westinghouse-Armature, sought to create a "fun" motif by decorating the ceilings in the master bath with frescoes done originally for the Sistine Chapel by Michel "Michelangelo" Angelo and importing a working Hawaiian volcano to heat the pool, which was originally a lake in Switzerland. For the owners' two children (originally the children of a Nobel prize-winning

physicist and a world-renowned ballet dancer), who sleep in their own
wing, (originally Versailles), the de-
signers chose . . .

And so on. After you have read a few articles like this, you should have plenty of nifty
ideas for the kind of furniture you want, although of course, given your price range,
you will have to buy it at a store with a
name like Big Stu's Discount House of
Taste, where the dinette sets are made from
compressed oatmeal.

Besides money, the other thing you need is
time. Nobody has ever come up with a good
explanation as to why this is, but it takes
longer to obtain a piece of furniture than to
construct a suspension bridge. My theory is
that furniture is not actually built by human beings, but rather is *grown*, probably in
some intensely humid Third World nation
where they have giant furniture trees that
can take years to produce a single ottoman.
When you place your order for, let's say, a
teal love seat, the order is mailed via boat to
a furniture plantation, where a worker, who
speaks little English, frowns at it, wipes the

Harvesting furniture
in the Sudan.

sweat from his brow, straps on his machete,
and walks into the jungle. He halts briefly
as a ripe armoire thuds into the earth ahead
of him, then he continues along the narrow
path, squinting upward into the dense mass
of vegetation overhead. He spots a dark
shape far above him in the gloom; it could be
a love seat in the early stages of formation.
Or it could be a coffee table, or a Barca-
lounger, or a gorilla nest. "Who knows?" the
worker thinks to himself. "And what the hell
is 'teal'?"

So we're talking about a slow and inexact
process, with one piece arriving years after
another, which is why most people go
through their entire lives without having all
their furniture look nice at the same time.
My advice is, order your furniture *now*,

even if you don't even own a house yet, even if you are in fact an unborn child, because if you are lucky, the last piece will arrive just in time for your great-great-grandchildren to spill Zoo-Roni on it. Not that you will care: you will hate it anyway. This is because of:

NEWTON'S FIRST LAW OF FURNI-TURE BUYING: The amount you will hate a given piece of furniture is equal to its cost multiplied by the length of time, in months, it takes to arrive.

I recall the time my wife, Beth, finally got fed up with the brown sofa we had for many years, which looked like a buffalo that had staggered into our living room and died from a horrible skin disease. So she decided, the hell with our son's college education, she was going to get a new sectional sofa. She took many measurements, then she went to many, many furniture stores, then she ordered the sofa, then we waited through several presidential administrations for it to arrive. And finally it did, and it was *exactly* what she had ordered, and so naturally it made her almost physically ill to look at it. I told her it looked fine to me, but it was no use. When she was looking at this sofa, she was looking at Jabba the Hutt. She would lie awake in bed at night, thinking about this *thing* squatting out there in her living room, and it was only a matter of time before she went insane and attacked it with a steak knife. So I was very relieved when she decided to sell it through a classified ad, which was a pretty interesting experience in itself because of the call she got from the sex maniac. This is the truth. First he asked her a bunch of questions about the sofa, which he seemed sincerely interested in, and then, lowering his voice about two octaves, he said:

"Are you wearing loafers?"

Beth failed to notice anything particularly unusual about this, which shows how crazed a person can become when she is desperate to get rid of a sectional sofa.

"Yes," she said. "Now, the sofa—"

"Are they brown?" he asked.

"Yes," she said. "But about the—"

"Do they *smell bad*?" he asked.

At this point Beth, even in her furniture-induced derangement, realized that this person was not a Hot Prospect, and she got off the phone. Eventually she sold the sofa, so it wasn't such a bad experience after all, though it probably would have been easier and more relaxing if we had just gone out into the backyard and set fire to a small pile of hundred-dollar bills.

Of course there is a way to obtain nice furniture without the frustration and high cost of buying it new, provided you are willing to put in a few hours of honest "elbow grease" and possibly suffer permanent disfigurement. I am referring, of course, to the time-honored Thrifty Homeowner art of . . .

REFINISHING FURNITURE

No doubt you have at one time or another visited the home of people who have a number of nice older wooden pieces, and you have said something complimentary, and your hosts said something like: "Oh, thank you, we bought them all for a total of $147.50 at garage sales and refinished them ourselves in the garage and now they are worth, we conservatively estimate, nine million dollars." They are lying, of course. They stole all this stuff from the Museum of Nice Old Wood Furniture. Nevertheless, it is inevitable that at some point you will get the notion that *you* can have nice furniture via the refinishing method, so you might as well know the correct procedure:

1. You go to a garage sale and you find a bureau covered with hideously ugly orange paint.
2. You call your spouse over, and you say, in a quiet voice so the garage sale person can't overhear you: "Look at this! You know what this is, under this paint? This is (CHOOSE ONE):
   ... solid oak!"
   ... solid bird's-eye maple!"
   ... solid walnut!"
   ... solid oaken maple eye of walnut!"
   (It makes no difference what fine hardwood you claim the bureau is made of, because it will forever remain an elusive dream that you never actually lay eyes on, similar to the Lost Dutchman's Mine.)

3. Your spouse, shocked, whispers: "Whoever would be so foolish as to cover up such beautiful wood with *paint*!? With a minimum of effort, this could be a *lovely* piece!"

4. Feeling like thieves in the night, you pay twenty-five dollars for the bureau and scuttle off with it. You do not hear the cynical laughter of the former owner.

5. You go to the hardware store and purchase some steel wool and some refinishing product with a name like "Can o' Poison" that has skeleton heads all over it and a prominent Consumer Advisory like this:

WARNING—DO NOT LET THIS PRODUCT COME IN CONTACT WITH YOUR SKIN. DO NOT BREATHE THE FUMES. DO NOT HAVE CHILDREN AFTER USING THIS PRODUCT. DO NOT BUY THIS PRODUCT. DO NOT EVEN READ THIS WARNING.

6. You go home, put on some rubber gloves, and start scrubbing the paint

with the toxic substance. It is hard work. It is dirty work. The gloves dissolve quickly, and it is clear that large patches of your skin will have to be surgically replaced. But it's all worth it, because after just a few hours you have scraped away a small patch of that hideous orange paint, and underneath it you find . . . *a layer of hideous green paint!*

7. You repeat this process for two, maybe even three more layers of paint, and finally the truth dawns on you: *This is not really a bureau.* This is an enormous, bureau-shaped wad of paint.

8. You decide to hold a garage sale.

INTERIOR DESIGN HINTS FROM TOP "PROS"

- To make a dark room look brighter, try turning on the electrical lights.
- A small carpet stain where the cat vomited in 1979 can be made to "disappear"

Interior Decorating
Hint:

How to make a dark room
look lighter

when company comes by having a predetermined family member stand on it and refuse to move.

- Squares of corkboard stuck on the wall will often turn an "ordinary" room into a room that smells like corkboard.

- If you're planning to paint a room, remember that "oil-based" paint is the kind that is supposed to come off with paint thinner, but does not; whereas "latex" is the kind that is supposed to come off with simple soap and water, but does not.

8

Good Housekeeping, or Learning to Live with Filth

Hardly a week goes by when you don't read a newspaper article like this:

LOS REDUNDOS, N.M.—Astronomers at the Institute for Wearing White Laboratory Coats here announced today that they have discovered a humongous dust cloud 237 skillion light-years from the earth. "This," the scientists stated in unison, "could very well be the largest dust cloud we have discovered since the one we discovered last week, and we believe that it may provide us with valuable insights into the mystery of how we can obtain additional federal grants."

What scientists are learning, through these dramatic breakthrough discoveries, is something that many of us have suspected for a long time, namely that the universe is made up almost entirely of dirt. More and more, scientists are suspecting that the Big Bang was in fact the explosion of a small but very densely packed vacuum cleaner bag.

So we must accept the fact that we live in a universe swarming with particles of filth that are ceaselessly trying to get into our homes and inflict themselves upon us, similar to insurance salespersons, but in some cases even more distasteful. Hard to believe? I thought so, too, until a short while back, when the people who publish the *Allergy Relief Newsletter* were thoughtful enough to send me, at their own expense, a piece of junk mail stating that my entire household was teeming with tiny dirt creatures named "dust mites," which sound like harmless and friendly commercially licensed characters such as might have their own Saturday morning cartoon show sponsored by the sugar industry, until you look at the photograph showing a dust mite enlarged several thousand times, and it looks exactly like the kind of hostile giant mutant insect that was always destroying Tokyo in those movies that the Japanese used to make before they figured out how to do cars. According to the folks at the *Allergy Relief Newsletter*, these dust mites are swarming everywhere, including *inside your nose*, millions of them per nostril. And although they are, fortunately, a peaceful species, not generally known to attack humans except during mating season, we need to be aware of them, because they serve as a constant nasal reminder of our central point, which, as best we can remember, is: There is a *lot* of dirt around.

What this means is that you, as a homeowner, have to make a decision: Are you going to let the dirt overcome you, so that you live your life encrusted by a permanent layer of greasy yellowish filth, so that you are no better than slugs writhing in their own putrid slime? Or are you going to make the commitment, in time, in effort, to fighting back—to really trying to keep your new home neat and tidy?

I have tried it both ways, and trust me, the writhing slug approach is better. You don't think important people, such as members of the U.S. Supreme Court, waste time cleaning, do you? Of course not! Their homes are filthy. *They* are filthy. That's why they wear those robes: they have whole tribes of dust mites under there. Because they have learned, like so many other people, that if you really, seriously try to keep your house clean, you gradually turn into one of those TV commercial housewives who are always frowning with grave concern at their bathroom bowls and having conversations like this with their friends:

FIRST HOUSEWIFE: Whatever is the matter, Sue?

SECOND HOUSEWIFE: Oh, Betty, I am so very upset because Waxy Yellow Buildup has caused my kitchen floor to look like some kind of gigantic nasal discharge!

FIRST HOUSEWIFE: Lordy yes, it does.

SECOND HOUSEWIFE: And Bob is bringing home the archbishop tonight!! Whatever shall I do?!

FIRST HOUSEWIFE: If it was me, I would take a major credit card and fly to the Caribbean island of Antigua and drink for days with strange men.

SECOND HOUSEWIFE: That is what I was thinking.

So we see that it can lead to bad things, this obsession some people have with housecleaning. What you want to do, in your household, is adopt the cleaning system my wife and I use, which is based on the old philosophical question: "If a tree falls in the forest, and nobody is there to hear it, does it make any sound?" (The answer, by the way, is yes; the tree goes: "Moo.") Our theory is, if there is nobody besides ourselves around to see the dirt, then *the dirt isn't really there*. So Rule Number One of successful housecleaning is:

>Never Let Anybody into Your House<

Not even your mother. *Especially* not your mother. I cannot overemphasize the importance of this rule. Even if you know some really nice people who have had you over to their house thirty-seven times for dinner, you must not weaken and invite them to your house. You must give them plausible excuses, such as: "We sincerely intend to have you folks over one of these days, but right now we're all in a dither because our housekeeper has been killed by radon gas."

Rule Number Two of successful housecleaning, of course, is:

> Never Have Children of Any Kind <

Each of us, as a human being, has an important choice to make: We can either experience the trials, the joys, the tragedies, and the triumphs of that most sacred of human institutions, parenthood; or we can have a house where we do not regularly find gerbil poop in our sofa. But we cannot have both of

Keeping your house clean.

these things. Because small children have no concept whatsoever of cleanliness. A small child's concept of housekeeping is to lick spilled pudding off the living room carpet. And it does not get better as they get older. For example, my son, now age seven, is in the phase where he likes to play with educational "construction" toys, designed by escaped Nazis, that consist of 363,000,000,000,000 tiny plastic pieces in a box. The way you play with these toys is, you strew the pieces all over the living room floor, and then you go outside to play. And when your mother yells: "Robert! Come in here and pick up your construction set!" you yell back: "I'm still *using* them!" And then late that night, you lie awake in bed, waiting for the moment when your father, heading for the kitchen to get a glass of orange juice, wanders out into the darkened living room and steps, barefooted, on the plastic pieces, which is the cue for him to perform the comically entertaining Midnight Dance of the Bozo Father, a rapid series of hopping, skating movements across the floor accompanied by whimpering, followed by very bad words. This is a good time for you to look like you are Sound Asleep.

Also your children will gradually cause your brain to become damaged in such a way that you deliberately engage in acts of antihousekeeping. For example, I once, at my son's insistence, spent perfectly good U.S. dollars at Toys Backwards "R" Us for a can of something called "Slime," which I naturally assumed was a toy but which in fact turned out to be exactly what its name suggests, namely, slime. Of course my son got it all over everything, and of course it wouldn't come off. My point being that, here we are living in a house that already seems to have a lifetime inexhaustible supply of natural dirt, and yet for some boneheaded parental reason I felt the need to go out and purchase *more* dirt.

An even worse example was the time my wife went out and bought mice. Of course the pet store people did not tell her they were mice. They are much too smart for that. They told her she was buying "gerbils," which, according to the instruction manual they also sold her, are a kind of "small desert animal found in Asia and Africa." But what they clearly are, when you look at them, is mice. I bet the folks over in Asia and Africa are tickled pink that we're willing to purchase their surplus vermin. They're probably wondering what kind of handsome price they might be able to get over here for their head lice.

I want to stress that my wife did not purchase merely the mice. No sir, because your mice also need food, and medical supplies, and of course *exercise equipment*, because

God forbid that they should become out of shape! They might get sick! You probably do not appreciate the extreme irony dripping from my word processor here, because chances are you were not in bed with me the night my wife came racing in and announced that there was mouse poop among the cereal boxes, and consequently we had to make an urgent call to the Lethal Chemicals Man. We live in South Florida, and like everybody else down here, we pay a man to come around regularly and spray the interior of our house with massive quantities of chemicals of the type that, if they were accidentally sprayed on our house by a major corporation, we would sue it for $350 million.

We do this to keep nature from coming inside. There is a tremendous amount of nature down here in South Florida, and despite our efforts to control it by covering it up as much as possible with condominiums, it is still a constant threat. I am not talking about the warm, furry kind of nature with big brown eyes that gets featured in animated motion pictures, scampering around collecting nuts for the winter and talking in high, squeaky voices. That is not what we have down here. Down here we have toads that can *kill* a person. I am serious. This is one of the first possibilities the police consider when they arrive at a murder scene.

FIRST POLICEMAN: This looks like the work of toads.

SECOND POLICEMAN: Why do you say that?

FIRST POLICEMAN: The victim's fly is missing!

SECOND POLICEMAN: Ha ha!

But it is no laughing matter, the nature problem down here. Even as I write these words, there is a spider right outside my house that could serve, all by itself, as our NATO forces. This spider has erected a web that covers most of our property and contains wrapped-up food bundles the size of missing neighborhood dogs.

So anyway, I find it highly ironic that we are paying the Lethal Chemicals Man to place deadly violent traps all around the Rice Krispies in hopes of sending *one* set of rodents to the Great Piece of Cheese in the Sky, while at the same time we are spending

otherwise useful money on *another* set of rodents, so they can have toys and Ferris wheels and God knows what else. Technically we are doing this for Educational Purposes, because Robert is eager to learn the Secrets of the Animal Kingdom, but these rodents don't *know* any secrets of the animal kingdom. All they know how to do is gnaw cardboard toilet paper tubes, which my son saves for them—heaven forbid I should throw one out—into 650,000 tiny pieces, which they then push out of their cage onto the floor. They do this very industriously, pretending they are engaging in the kind of serious life-or-death tasks that animals engage in on TV nature specials, but in fact they do it solely because they know it really frosts my shorts.

"Look," they say to each other, in Rodent. "He's cleaning it up again! Ha ha! This is a LOT more fun than Africa and Asia!"

They'll change *that* tune when we get the Educational Cat.

Which reminds us of another important housekeeping rule . . .

> Never Have a Dog <

Let's not beat around the bush here: dogs are morons. Don't get me wrong: I *like* dogs. We have always had dogs, and they have faithfully performed many valuable services for us, such as:

1. Peeing on everything.
2. When we're driving in our car, alerting us that we have passed another dog by bark-

ing real loud in our ears for the next 114 miles.

3. Trying to kill the Avon lady.

Very Small Things:

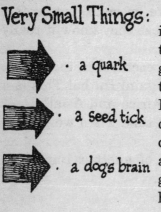

· a quark

· a seed tick

· a dog's brain

But despite their instinctive skills in these areas, dogs generally rank, on the Animal Kingdom IQ Scale, somewhere down in the paramecium range, and they above all do *not* grasp the concept of housekeeping. Show me a household with a dog in it, and I will show you a household with numerous low-altitude wall stains where the dog, rounding a corner at several hundred miles per hour in an effort to get to the front door and welcome the master home by knocking the master down, whammed into the wall and left a brownish smear of whatever repulsive substance it was rolling in earlier that day.

Discipline will not prevent this kind of thing. You can sit a dog down and explain to it very carefully that you just purchased a new oriental rug, and you don't want the dog to go anywhere *near* it. You can point to the rug and go "NO!" a dozen times, and the dog will look at you with an extremely alert and intelligent expression, similar to the way Lassie always looked when she was piloting a helicopter somewhere to rescue her young cretin master Jeff, who had fallen into the quicksand again. Then your dog will go outside and sprint around in concentric circles until it has found a rancid, maggot-festooned sector of deceased raccoon. It will race back to your house with this prize as though the fate of the Free World depended on it, deposit it on your rug, and wander off to take a well-earned nap.

USEFUL HOME-CLEANING HINTS

- If your child draws pictures of cows on your woodwork with a felt-tipped marker, you can scrub them with a mixture of one part baking soda, one part lemon juice, and one part ammonia, but they won't come off.

- The best way to clean a frying pan that has burned food cemented to the bottom is to let it soak in soapy water for several days and then, when nobody is looking, throw it in the garbage.
- If you ever find the person who invented "Slime," call me and I will come over and plug up all the orifices in his head with a mixture of one part Tabasco sauce and one part Play-Doh.
- Many smart homemakers such as Cher and Queen Elizabeth have found that the best way to "stay ahead" of those pesky household "chores" is to have a "staff."
- Ever wonder how come the males in your household pee everywhere except into the actual toilet bowl? It's because they are jerks.

9

Practical Home Weapons Systems

One of our major responsibilities, as home-owners, is to become needlessly alarmed about home security. And with good reason. All we have to do is look at the front page of our newspaper, and we will see frightening headlines such as the following:

BOY RAISED BY CHICKENS ET SPACE ALIEN CURED MY ACNE GIRL, 2, GIVES BIRTH WHILE SKYDIVING

Okay, perhaps we should be reading a better class of newspaper. But the point is, there are grave threats all around us, and we need to be ready.

I happen to be an expert in the area of home security, because I live in South Florida, home of Miami Vice, where guns are extremely easy to obtain. Down here they give you a free revolver when you buy a Big Gulp at the 7-Eleven. So you have a lot of people walking around armed, the result being that a lot of homeowners feel that they, too, need to arm themselves in self-defense. Of course your bleeding-heart-liberal-secular-

HOME SECURITY

1. Your Gun:

2. A Safe Place to Put It:

140

humanist left-wing communists will tell you that it's a bad thing to own a gun, but as any knowledgeable gun nut will tell you, there are countless factual anecdotes concerning alert gun-toting homeowners who have thwarted the forces of evil.

For example, we recently had a case here where a homeowner woke up at 2:30 A.M. because he thought he had heard a noise in the family room. Grabbing his revolver, he slowly opened his bedroom door and crept stealthily into the darkened hallway, where he stepped barefooted onto a cockroach— down here we get cockroaches large enough to derail trains—causing him (the homeowner) to leap straight into the air and shoot his gun, the bullet from which went through the wall and into the garage, where it hit the circuit breaker box and cut off the electrical power to the house, thus shutting down the videocassette recorder in the family room, where the homeowner's eleven-year-old son had been watching *Debbie Does Dallas*. So don't try to tell *me* that guns have no place in the home. Don't try to tell it to the Founding Fathers of this nation, either. For one thing, they are dead. For another thing, they specifically considered the question of guns when they wrote the Constitution, and after much debate, they agreed on the following unequivocal wording regarding the right of the people to keep and bear arms:

ARTICLE XMZXMZBX: If guns were outlaws, then outlaws would be guns.

So you can play it any way you want it, but this is one homeowner whose motto is: "You can have my gun when you threaten to pry one of my fingers off the trigger."

Of course, if you *do* get a gun, you need to follow certain basic safety procedures, such as:

1. Don't keep it loaded.
2. Don't even have the proper caliber of bullet for it.
3. Keep it someplace safe, such as a safe-deposit box in Switzerland.

What other steps can you take to protect yourself? One approach that combines the advantage of costing a lot of money with the advantage of really ticking off your neighbors is . . .

THE ELECTRONIC BURGLAR
ALARM SYSTEM

Essentially, this is a complex system of modern, sophisticated, state-of-the-art, fully computerized components, costing no more than several semesters at Stanford University graduate school, yet giving you the sense of security and well-being that comes from knowing that everyone in your neighborhood will be instantly alerted by a horrible ear-splitting noise whenever lightning strikes anywhere within 137 miles of your home. Invariably this will happen at night when you're out of town, so that your neighbors will get to lie in bed, listening to the piercing sound, which is only fair because it makes up for all the nights when *you* had to listen to *their* burglar alarm systems.

I do not mean to suggest that burglar alarm systems go off only when lightning strikes. No, they also go off when the electric company has problems, or when homeowners forget to turn them off upon returning. Sometimes birds set them off. "Let's go set off some burglar alarms!" is a cry frequently heard among adolescent finches. Even air molecules, which are plentiful in the suburbs, can set off burglar alarm systems. In fact, the only thing that *doesn't* set them off, as far as we can tell, is burglars. Nobody can explain this phenomenon, but police rely on it when they go on their patrols. They'll drive through a neighborhood at 4 A.M., listening to three or four home security systems electronically whooping and shrieking into the night, and they'll say to each other, using hand signals so they can be understood over the din: "Everything's fine here!"

Of course these systems are not perfect. Even the most well-designed electronic device cannot be relied upon to go off without any reason one hundred percent of the time. Thus most security experts also recommend that you have a backup system consisting of . . .

A LARGE, STUPID DOG

I realize that in the chapter on housecleaning I specifically said you should never have a dog, on the grounds that they are filthy, but my feeling, as a professional author, is that if I go through life worrying about what I may have said in previous chapters, I will never get anything done. So in this chapter, I am strongly in favor of dogs as security devices, but I stress that they must be *large*. You don't want one of those repulsive little yapping "lap"-style dogs that look like fur-covered insects, because the burglar will simply stuff it down the garbage disposal. This is fine as far as it goes, but it doesn't do you any good, home-securitywise. What you want is a major hunk of canine muscle, the kind that is always on Full Red Alert, the kind that will race to the front door, barking violently, when it hears any sound, including its own parasites.

We are blessed with such a dog, Earnest, and she is a source of great comfort to us, for we know that as long as we have her, our home is totally protected from Zachary

Electronic Home Security System:

Backup System:

Liebman, age five. This is the little boy who lives next door and comes over to play with our son. Earnest absolutely hates him. When we moved in, Earnest received signals from whatever distant planet it is that dogs get their instructions from, and these signals told her that Zachary Liebman is the most dangerous creature in the galaxy, and there is nothing we can do to change her mind. Zachary has come over to our house almost daily for two years now, and still she follows him around, emitting a constant low growl to let him know that she is ready in case he suddenly pulls out a concealed machine gun. And so of course we have to follow *her* around, going "NO! Earnest, NO!!" although this has no effect, because in matters of home security, Earnest takes orders only from the Dog Planet. So we form a colorful and loud procession—Zachary, oblivious; Earnest, furious; and my wife or me, slowly going hoarse—parading around the house, sometimes for hours. You can't put a price on this kind of piece of mind.

ONE FINAL WORD ABOUT
HOME SECURITY

None of the security methods we have discussed here will foil the truly determined burglar, the veteran professional who has already broken into hundreds of homes just like yours and has been convicted seventeen times and is currently out of jail on his own recognizance. The best you can hope for, with any security method, is that you will make your home look slightly less attractive to the burglar, so that he'll pass you and burglarize somebody else's house. In fact, you might leave a little note on your door, letting the burglar know that your particular house is probably less attractive to him than several other homes in your neighborhood where you know for a fact that the owners are away on vacation. Sure, this means extra work for you, but society has no chance against the Criminal Element if people like yourself aren't willing to "get involved."

CRIMESTOPPER TIPS

- If you go away for any length of time, be sure to leave a radio on in your house tuned to a station that plays "rap" music, so that if a burglar does get in, most of his brain cells will be killed instantly and he won't be able to remember how to get back out.
- Also, you should ask a neighbor to come around and collect your mail and your newspapers, put out your garbage, and while he's at it, maybe mow your lawn and paint your house and build a deck out back. Hey, it's worth a shot.

10

A Lawn Is a Terrible Thing
to Waste

Up to this point we have been concentrating on the inside of your house, because that's where you actually live, unless you are even dumber than we thought. But the *outside* of your house—the grounds and how they are landscaped—is also important, especially in terms of property values. To illustrate this point, let's consider two homeowners, whom we'll call "Smith" and "Jones." (These are not their real names. Their real names are "Smith" and "Brown.") Let's say these two people bought identical homes in the same neighborhood on the same day for the same price, fifty-thousand dollars.

"Smith," a very hard worker, takes excellent care of his yard. Every weekend he's out there mowing his lawn, pruning his shrubs, and crouching in the dirt working on his flower beds. Meanwhile "Jones" is a lazy lout who never does anything to his property except occasionally empty his car ashtray on it on his way to the convenience store to buy more beer.

Now, let's say that at the end of five years, both properties are placed on the market. "Jones," who failed to maintain his yard, gets $72,500 for his property. This price, when adjusted for inflation, works out to be a profit of just 7.2 percent for our lazy homeowner. But "Smith," the hard worker, would have received $86,300 for his property, if he had not been attacked by fire ants one afternoon while he was weeding the pachysandra patch and stung an estimated five-hundred-thousand times before his body was found by the water softener man, who later married "Smith's" widow, who was able to use the life insurance money to buy them a luxury condominium where the closest they ever come to yard work is sometimes they fling the ice from their gin and tonic off their balcony onto the golf course. So there should be no question in your mind about the value of properly maintaining your property.

The key area, of course, is the lawn. This is the centerpiece of the yard, and it has been for hundreds of years, ever since the invention of . . .

THE VERY FIRST LAWN

Like so many other good ideas, such as eating snails, the lawn was invented by a French person, Jean-Harold Discotheque, in 1732. He called his invention "L'awn" (French for "the awn"). His prototype lawn was very primitive, consisting of only one humongous blade of grass about 30 feet in diameter and 120 feet high; so, as you can imagine, it was not ideal for such purposes as croquet, plus it was hell to mow. But in the following years there were a number of spectacular technical breakthroughs—the two-blades-of-grass lawn; the six-blades-of-grass lawn; etc.—until finally we reached the modern lawn consisting of many millions of tiny blades, each one of them diseased. This is where we stand today.

THE FUTURE: LAWNS IN SPACE

Currently there are no lawns in space, although the U.S. Defense Department Office of Massive Stupid Wasteful Projects has a crash program to put one there before the Russians do. As you can imagine, this is an exceedingly difficult task, for space is a very hostile environment almost totally devoid of mulch.

LAWN CARE IN AMERICA

We Americans can make the proud boast that no other nation cares for its lawns as much as we do. Lawn care has made America what it is today, as can be shown by this chart:

UNITED STATES		JAPAN	
	•••	•••	
	•••	•••	
	•••	•••	
	•••	•••	
	•••	•••	
	•••	•••	
	•••	•••	
	•••	•••	
•••	•••	•••	•••
•••	•••	•••	•••
•••	•••	•••	•••
Industrial Productivity	Time Spent on Lawn Care	Industrial Productivity	Time Spent on Lawn Care

As a patriotic noncommunist homeowner, you are responsible for maintaining the American tradition of lawn care and learning as much as you can about this important subject from books other than this one. You definitely won't find anything useful here. I care for my lawn about as well as Godzilla cared for Tokyo. When I die, I will go to Lawn Hell, where homeowners like myself are forced to lie outside with no food or water and have dogs pee on them while their lawns relax inside on Barcaloungers, eating barbecue chips and watching football on TV.

Nevertheless, I have, over the years, learned a few basic facts about lawn care, the two major ones being:

Proper Lawn Care:

Car Ashtray

Lawn

Driveway

- If you fail to feed, fertilize, and water your lawn, it will die.
- If you feed, fertilize, and water your lawn, it will die.

Fortunately this is not a problem, because you can always get a new lawn, in the form of "sod." The way sod works is, you pay a large sum of money, and sweaty men arrive at your house driving a filthy truck, on the back of which is stacked an actual living, breathing, feeling lawn, Some Assembly Required. God only knows where the sweaty men *get* this lawn. My theory is that they simply go and steal somebody *else's* lawn, so that over the course of several decades, the same lawn could make its way, house by house, through an entire subdivision.

PROPER LAWNMOWER CARE

It's important to take good care of your lawnmower, because as the old yard care saying goes: "A lawnmower that is running right is a lawnmower that is capable of slic-

Lawnmower Maintenance:
Looking for the Sparkplug Fairy

ing through your foot like a machete through Wonder bread." This is why manufacturers recommend that you perform the following routine maintenance procedure on your lawnmower every two weeks or ten-thousand miles, whichever comes first.

1. Lubricate the linkage connecting the abatement disk to the invective moderator, taking care not to masticate the tropism extractor.
2. Remove the parameter valve from the heliotrope converter and examine the reversion unit for signs of fatigue or drowsiness.
3. Let's not kid ourselves. You're not really going to follow this maintenance proce-

dure, right? I bet you never engage in *any* of the Goody-Two-Shoes consumer activities that manufacturers are always recommending. Me either. Like, whenever I buy an electronic product, the first thing I do is remove the safety information sheet that says, "URGENT EMERGENCY ALERT: BEFORE YOU ATTEMPT TO USE THIS PRODUCT, PLEASE PLEASE *PLEASE* FOR GOD'S SAKE IF YOU VALUE YOUR LIFE READ THIS SAFETY INFORMATION SHEET," and I toss that baby right into the trash compactor. I would no more perform routine maintenance procedures on my lawnmower than I would clean my barbecue grill, or inspect my air conditioner filter, or save my original appliance cartons, or wipe my telephone answering machine with a damp cloth, or any of the other 1,536,862 idiotic things that various manufacturers, in an effort to turn me into a mindless consumer geek, have recommended that I do. Because this is America. This is the land of rugged, independent, self-reliant freedom fighters like Davy Crockett, who stood tall at the Alamo and fought on bravely even though he and his small band of men were badly outnumbered by thousands of manufacturers, coming over the walls in waves, armed to the teeth with Limited Warranties. And I am proud to say that the same spirit still exists today, that people like yourself and myself deal with lawnmower maintenance the way Americans have dealt with it since the Revolutionary War, namely: We leave our lawnmowers unattended in the garage all winter, and then we drag them out, brush off the spiders and yank fruitlessly on the cord until we are about two yanks shy of cardiac arrest; then we remove the spark plug and peer into the little hole, hoping that maybe the Spark Plug Fairy will appear in there and wave her tiny wand and make everything okay, but of course she doesn't, so we hurl the lawnmower into our car and drive down to the lawnmower repair place, where they tell us that it will be two to three months before they can even give us an estimate, because of the large backlog caused by other rugged and self-reliant homeowners like our-selves.

SHRUBS

Shrubs are pathetic little mutant trees that you purchase to replace the nice big trees that were probably on your property before the developer came in and knocked them over with bulldozers. The way you plant a shrub is, you and your spouse lug it around your yard, setting it here and there and then standing back to see how it looks, until you settle on a spot directly over the largest buried boulder on your property, which is where you start digging. Shrub-lugging homeowners are so effective at locating buried objects that they are now routinely employed by archaeological expeditions. The archaeologist will get a couple from, say, Milwaukee, take them over to Egypt, hand them a juniper bush, and ask them where they think it should be planted. Then, using a helicopter, he'll follow them as they wander around the endless, undifferentiated

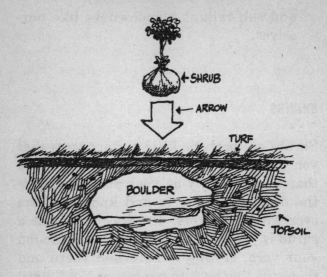

Correct Placement
of Shrubbery

desert for days, plopping their shrub here
and there, looking at it, shaking their heads,
and moving on. When, finally, they're satisfied that they've found the right spot, the archaeologist will swoop down, stick his shovel
into the sand, and—CLUNK—there will be
the sound of metal striking an ancient tomb
that has lain undisturbed for four-thousand
years. It saves a lot of time.

GARDENING

Americans have never been as fond of gardening as, for example, the British, who have, through centuries of puttering, managed to transform their little island into one of the world's fourth-rate powers. Of course you cannot hope to achieve this kind of result in your own yard, but you will definitely find that for every hour you spend tilling the soil in the early spring, you will be richly rewarded with many more hours of fertilizing the soil in the late spring and weeding the soil all summer.

There are many different types of gardens to choose from, such as the flower garden, which consists of flowers; the vegetable garden, which consists of vegetables; and the

The English Garden: OR, HOW TO TURN YOUR BACKYARD INTO A FOURTH-RATE WORLD POWER.

Japanese garden, which consists of Japanese. But I myself have found that the best type, in terms of ease of maintenance, is the "garden consisting of ugly plaster statuettes." Of course the type of ugly statuette you should choose depends on the climate in your particular area.

Ugly Concrete Statuettes for the Garden:

Climate	Correct type of statuette
Warm	Burro
Cold	Cat
Humid	Toadstool
Tasteless	Religious

11

Getting Some Fool to Buy Your House

No matter how perfect your new home seems when you first move in, you'll gradually discover various shortcomings about it that get on your nerves, and ultimately you'll come to hate it. This usually takes about two weeks. From that point on, you'll be thinking about Trading Up.

Trading Up is the basic maneuver in real

Trading Up

estate, dating back several million years to the prehistoric Catalytic Era. In those days, a typical couple would have to start out living in a small cave, but each day they'd go out and hunt for pretty stones, which they'd put in a pile, called Equity, in the center of their cave. When the Equity was big enough, they'd move to a larger cave, where they'd repeat the process and move to a still larger one, and so on until they moved into their Dream Cave, which was occupied by a saber-toothed tiger, or *carnivorous humongous* (literally, "huge payments"), which ate them. This is essentially the system we use today.

Before you can buy a new house, of course, you need to sell the one you're in now.

THE BEST WAY TO SELL A HOUSE

The best way to sell a house is to walk down a city street and have a construction worker who is eating a sandwich fifty-five stories above you accidentally drop his lunch box so that it lands on your head in such a way that you are not seriously injured, but you do lapse into a coma, and you wake up four months later and the nurse says: "While you were in a coma, your house was sold." This is also the best way to move, have a baby, and attend the opera. But things are rarely this easy. Usually you have to put quite a bit of effort into selling your house, starting with asking yourself the question . . .

DO YOU NEED A REAL ESTATE BROKER?

I touched upon this subject back in an earlier chapter, but I am quite frankly too lazy to go back and read what I said. Probably I said that there are pros and cons, because there almost always are, unless you're talking about hemorrhoidal tissue.

169

On the one hand, if you sell your home yourself, you avoid paying a large commission; but on the other hand, you have to deal with people calling you up and coming around to your house all hours of the day and night, pestering you and giving you no peace. I'm not talking about potential buyers. I'm talking about real estate brokers, trying to get your listing. The only way to get them to go away is to sign a contract with them. Then you'll never see them again.

Ha ha! Just kidding, of course. In the interest of fairness and decency and, above all, not receiving thousands of concerned letter bombs from the large and powerful real estate industry, let me state that I am sure that virtually all brokers out there are honest and highly competent professionals of the type regularly shown on TV wearing geek-style blazers. And even if it turns out that they're not, I strongly advise you to use a broker, for the same reason that I'd advise you to pay somebody else to repair your automobile transmission, namely: No matter how incompetent or overpaid this person is, he or she can't possibly screw things up as badly as you would if you did it yourself.

Before you sign a listing contract, you should talk to several brokers, to find out what they think your house is worth. What you want to be on the alert for here is a practice called "highballing," which is when an unscrupulous broker deliberately overestimates the value of your house, just to get the listing:

BROKER: Mr. and Mrs. Jones, based on thoroughly walking around your living room here, I would estimate that the market value of your house is a hillion gazillion dollars.

YOU (suspiciously): Wait a minute. *Our* name isn't Jones.

BROKER: Don't worry about that. This is just a pretend dialogue in a humor book.

Once you've selected a broker, you'll be asked to sign a standard contract, which will read as follows:

STANDARD REAL ESTATE LISTING AGREEMENT

1. The BROKER gets FIVE PERCENT.
2. Even if the BROKER doesn't do SQUAT.
3. Even if the BROKER is off somewhere like MAUI, drinking EXOTIC TROPICAL DRINKS with names like KAMIKAZE KAHLUA when a WILLING BUYER, acting totally on his OWN, appears on the SELLER'S doorstep carrying a SUITCASE full of CASH MONEY, the BROKER still gets FIVE PERCENT.
4. In return, the SELLER gets to bitch about the BROKER at social occasions.
5. "My damned BROKER couldn't sell mascara to TAMMY FAYE BAKKER," is the kind of snide comment the SELLER is allowed to make.
6. But the BROKER still gets FIVE PERCENT.

HOW MUCH SHOULD YOU
ASK FOR YOUR HOUSE?

This is a very difficult question, but top real estate experts from all over the world agree that you should ask $127,500 and ultimately settle for $119,250. Also you should throw in the outdoor gas barbecue system with the charcoal-roasted spiders permanently bonded to the grill.

GETTING YOUR HOUSE
READY TO SHOW

Once you're signed up with a broker and have decided on an asking price, you need to fix your house up so it looks as though clean and tasteful grownups live there, instead of yourselves. Take a hard look at your house and furnishings, and ask yourself how they'll appear to prospective buyers. Chances are that with a minimum of time and effort, you can make a number of dramatically superficial improvements. For example, suppose you have an ugly old sofa in the living room with a leg missing from one corner, which you've propped up with a copy of *The Sex Lusters*, by Harold Robbins. You'll make a far better impression with an acknowledged classic such as *Moby Dick*, by Jackie Collins. You can also make a big improvement in the appearance of dirty, crayon-marked walls by buying a can of flat white latex paint and using it to stand on while you install a lower-wattage light bulb.

Making your house presentable for sale:

No →

Yes →

And, of course, it's always a smart idea to nail all your bathroom doors shut.

The overall effect you're trying to create with these "homey" little touches is that your house is a warm, welcoming, and—above all—*real* kind of place, similar to the set of a 1962 situation comedy. You may want to create the impression that, at any moment, Ricky Ricardo might come bursting through the front door and get a great big welcome-home kiss from Mary Tyler Moore.

But the most important ingredient in the home-selling equation is *you*, the home-owner, because only you have a really intimate, detailed knowledge of the house; only you, who have lived there, know all the interesting little idiosyncrasies it has—all the special features and hidden "secrets" that make you want to dump it like a grocery bag full of armpit hair. Your job is to help your broker make sure that prospective buyers view these things in the proper light.

Unfortunately, brokers don't always appreciate receiving help from sellers. In fact, most brokers won't even want you hanging around when they show the house. They'll let you know this by dropping little hints such as: "Please don't hang around when I show the house," and: "If you hang around when I show the house, I will kill you." The broker is concerned that if you're always hovering in the background like some kind of desperate street person, the prospective buyers won't feel free to speak their minds.

There is some basis for the broker's concern. The last time we sold a house, whenever I was in the room, the prospective buyers would always describe everything as "interesting."

"Hmmmm," they say, looking at one of my Home Improvement Projects. "How interesting!" Meaning: "I can't *wait* to tell the people in my office about this."

So on the one hand, you don't want to make the buyers feel uncomfortable, but on the other hand, you want to be available to explain features of the home that the broker might not be familiar with. The solution to this dilemma is to *hide in closets* when prospective buyers come around. By ducking from room to room just ahead of them, you'll be invisible, yet still available in case a question comes up that the broker can't answer.

PROSPECTIVE BUYERS: What is this greenish slime dripping from the ceiling everywhere and eating holes in the floor?

BROKER: Well, it's, umm, errr, it's, ah . . .

VOICE FROM CLOSET: It's nothing to worry about!

PROSPECTIVE BUYERS (vastly relieved): Whew! Because for a moment there, we were concerned.

One major problem you'll have to be on the alert for is when prospective buyers get really interested in your house and start to bring around . . .

HORRIBLE RELATIVES

Virtually all prospective buyers have horrible relatives with names like Uncle Roger who believe themselves to be experts in the field of home construction on the basis of their vast experience as thirty-year subscribers to *Popular Mechanics*. The prospective buyers will bring Uncle Roger around, and unless he is stopped, he will go into

Handling the Buyer's
First offer

a testosterone-induced nitpicking frenzy
wherein he finds hundreds of thousands of
things wrong with your house. This is why
it's always a good idea, when you're darting
from closet to closet, to carry a garrote:

REAL ESTATE BROKER: And this is the master bedroom.

UNCLE ROGER: Well, this here is no good.
These windows are only double-glazed.
You want triple-glazed, plus you don't
want this kind of hinge. Plus you want

more electrical outlets than this. Plus you want AAAAACCCCCCCCCCKKK-KKK!

REAL ESTATE BROKER: What on earth was *that*?

PROSPECTIVE BUYERS: Somebody just jumped out of that closet over there and garroted Uncle Roger.

AUNT LOUISE: Good.

Sooner or later, if you continue to engage in savvy sales techniques such as these, a buyer will become interested enough to make an offer on your house. The important thing, during these negotiations, is to *remain calm*. Do *not* become emotionally involved. Remember that even though you and the buyers are on "opposite sides of the fence," the odds are that they are just regular everyday human beings like yourself, the only difference being that they're trying to screw you out of all your worldly goods. So while on the one hand you want to be reasonable, in the sense of frowning thoughtfully at the buyers' opening offer, you also want to be firm, in the sense of hurling it disdainfully to the floor and inviting friends and neighbors to help you spit on it.

Price is not the key issue in these negotiations. As I noted in an earlier chapter, the price you will ultimately settle on is the same one everybody always settles on, namely about five percent less than what you originally asked. Both sides know this, deep in their souls, but nobody really wants to just come out and admit it, for fear of appearing to be a wimp. So what you'll do—everybody does this—is get into serious, heavy-duty negotiations over which side gets to keep various home accessories such as:

- Ugly light fixtures
- Dingy draperies, and above all
- Minor grease-encrusted kitchen appliances that nobody really wants

These are the areas in which you want to be as petty as is humanly possible, in an effort to establish that you are a Tough Customer Who Will Not Be Taken Advantage Of. You want to stride in a forceful manner around your family room, cigar in hand, shouting instructions to your broker, such as:

"All right, they can have the Veg-O-Matic, but the sons of bitches are *not* gonna get the optional grape-peeling attachment!"

And:

"They want the *ice cube trays*?! Over MY DEAD BODY!!"

Using this aggressive approach, you should be able to retain possession of many of your prized home accessories, which will fetch you a handsome $1.85 when you hold your garage sale.

HOW YOU WILL FEEL AFTER YOU FINALLY SIGN THE AGREEMENT OF SALE

You'll experience a feeling of almost unbelievable elation, even better than the way you felt the time Geraldo Rivera opened Al Capone's vault on national TV and it was empty. This feeling will last for as long as seven tenths of a second, at which point you'll remember the clause in the sale agreement, put there by some writhing little insect of a lawyer, that states:

The SELLER agrees that if, at ANY TIME prior to the actual sale of the house, SOMETHING BAD happens, like for example let's say that on THE VERY MORNING OF THE SETTLEMENT, through NO FAULT OF THE SELLER, a TREE ROOT that for 127 years has been totally benign, suddenly, as if guided by DESTINY, decides to block the MAIN MUNICIPAL WASTEWATER LINE in front of the seller's house, causing a veritable VOLCANO OF RAW SEWAGE to erupt right in the SELLER'S GUEST BATHROOM and quickly flow THROUGHOUT THE ENTIRE HOUSE while the SELLER is out at the SUPERMARKET picking up a bottle of WINDEX so as to put the last few finishing touches on the HOUSE so that it will be neat as a PIN for the NEW OWNERS, then

HA HA the SELLER has to give the BUYER all his DEPOSIT MONEY back and the SELLER can kiss the whole deal GOOD-BYE.

So for the two months, or whatever, between the time you sign the contract and the time you actually close the deal, you'll experience a condition that famed psychologist Sigmund Freud identified as Agreement of Sale Paranoia. You'll be afraid to use the heating or air-conditioning systems; afraid to use the water faucets, turn on lights, or close doors firmly; afraid even to speak too loudly, for fear that you might set off some kind of sympathetic vibration that will cause the whole house to fall down. In short, you will become a crazy person. "YOU FOOL!" you'll shriek, leaping out from behind your hedge and tackling the UPS man just as he's about to ring your doorbell. "Are you trying to KILL US ALL?"

This is a natural reaction, but the truth is, you probably have nothing to worry about. The odds are that nothing bad will happen, and when you finally get to the Ritual Closing Ceremony, when you realize that the whole thing *is* going to work out after all, you'll experience a feeling of relief, a feeling that will grow stronger and stronger until, moments before the sale is legally finalized, you are knocked to the floor by the shock wave from the gas main exploding directly under your house.

But you're not going to let a little thing like the total destruction of your house, seconds before you were about to sell it, get you down. No, you are made of sterner stuff than that: you are a Homeowner. You're not a particularly *bright* one, given the fact that you bought this book, but nevertheless you are going to pick up the pieces of your life, as soon as they come down out of the sky, and get on with your life. Because you know that you'll have plenty more homes to own before you finally shuffle off what we in the real estate profession call "this mortal coil" and go up to that Great Subdivision in the Sky. I'm willing to bet there will be nothing in your price range.

Index

Available now in bookstores everywhere!

DAVE BARRY'S COMPLETE GUIDE TO GUYS

by Dave Barry

Published in hardcover by Random House

Turn the page for a sneak preview from Barry's outrageous new book . . .

INTRODUCTION
Guys vs. Men

This is a book about guys. It's *not* a book about men. There are already way too many books about men. Most of these books fall into one of two categories:

- **Anti-Men Books** declaring that men are oppressive, self-centered, testosterone-crazed scum who can't even commit themselves to an entire TV show, let alone a monogamous relationship; plus they tend to think that they're the only major gender capable of running large corporations and governmental institutions, despite the fact that the vast majority of them have never figured out how to do a load of laundry without having the underwear come out purple.
- **Pro-Men Books** declaring that men are, deep down inside, vibrant earthy spiritual beings who are capable of great sensitivity if they get back in touch with their inner selves via introspection and hugging and chanting and pounding on drums even though they may have no musical talent, let alone a bass player.

Don't get me wrong: These books are fine in their place, which is garage sales. The problem with them, in my opinion, is that they take men far too seriously. "Men" itself is a serious word, not to mention "manhood" and "manly." Such words make being male sound like a very important activity, as opposed to what it primarily consists of, namely, possessing a set of minor and frequently unreliable organs.

But men tend to attach great significance to Manhood. This results in certain characteristically masculine, by which I mean stupid, behavioral patterns that can produce unfortunate results such as violent crime, war, spitting, and ice hockey. These things have given males a bad name.[1] And the "Men's Movement," which is supposed to bring out the more positive aspects of Manliness, seems to be densely populated with loons and goobers.

So I'm saying that there's a third way to look at males: not as aggressive macho dominators; not as sensitive, liberated hugging drummers; but as *guys*.

And what, exactly, do I mean by "guys"? I don't know. I haven't thought that much about it. One of the major characteristics of guyhood is that we guys don't spend a lot of time pondering our deep, innermost feelings. There is a serious question in my mind about whether guys actually *have* deep innermost feelings, unless you count, for example, loyalty to the Detroit Tigers, or fear of bridal showers.

But although I can't define exactly what it means to be a guy, I can describe certain guy characteristics, such as:

GUYS LIKE NEAT STUFF.

By "neat," I mean "mechanical and unnecessarily complex." I'll give you an example. Right now I'm typing these words on an *extremely* powerful computer. It's the latest in a line of maybe ten computers I've owned, each one more powerful than the last. My computer is chockfull of RAM and ROM and bytes and megahertzes and various other items that enable a computer to kick data-processing butt. It is probably capable of supervising the entire U.S. air-defense apparatus while simultaneously

[1] Specifically, "asshole."

processing the tax return of every resident of Ohio. I use it mainly to write a newspaper column. This is an activity wherein I sit and stare at the screen for maybe ten minutes, then, using only my forefingers, slowly type something like:

Henry Kissinger looks like a big wart.

I stare at this for another ten minutes, have an inspiration, then amplify the original thought as follows:

Henry Kissinger looks like a big fat wart.

Then I stare at that for another ten minutes, pondering whether I should try to work in the concept of "hairy."

This is absurdly simple work for my computer. It sits there, humming impatiently, bored to death, passing the time between keystrokes via brain-teaser activities such as developing a Unified Field Theory of the universe and translating the complete works of Shakespeare into rap.[2]

In other words, this computer is absurdly overqualified to work for me, and yet soon, I guarantee, I will buy an *even more powerful* one. I won't be able to stop myself. I'll claim[3] that I need the new computer, but the truth is that I just *want* it. If there's a reason why I can't buy a computer for myself—say I've had my current one for less than a week—I'll try to talk my wife, Beth, an editor who can use the same computer for *years*, into getting a new one.

"Why?" she'll say. "Mine works fine."

Beth doesn't care about RAM *or* ROM.

Probably the ultimate example of the fundamental guy drive to have neat stuff is the Space Shuttle. Granted, the guys in charge of this program *claim* it has a Higher Scientific Purpose, namely to see how humans function in space. But of course we have known for years how humans function in space: They float around and say things like: "Looks real good, Houston!"

No, the real reason for the existence of the Space Shuttle is that it is one humongous and spectacularly gizmo-intensive item of hardware. Guys can tinker with it practically forever, and occasionally even get it to work,

[2] *To be or not? I got to KNOW.*
   Might kill myself by the end of the SHOW.
[3] Especially on my federal tax return.

190

and use it to place *other* complex mechanical items into orbit, where they almost immediately break, which provides a great excuse to send the Space Shuttle up *again*. It's Guy Heaven.

Other results of the guy need to have stuff are Star Wars, the recreational boating industry, monorails, nuclear weapons, and wristwatches that indicate the phase of the moon. I am not saying that women have not been involved in the development or use of this stuff. I'm saying that, without guys, this stuff probably would not exist; just as, without women, virtually every piece of furniture in the world would still be in its original position. Guys do not have a basic need to rearrange furniture. Whereas my wife, Beth, who happens to be a woman and who, as noted, would cheerfully use the same computer for fifty-three years, rearranges our furniture on almost a weekly basis, sometimes in the dead of night. She'll be sound asleep in bed, and suddenly, at 2 A.M., she'll be awakened by the urgent thought: *The blue-green sofa needs to go perpendicular to the wall instead of parallel, and it needs to go there RIGHT NOW.* So she'll get up and move it, which of course necessitates moving other furniture, and soon she has rearranged our entire living room, shifting great big heavy pieces that ordinarily would require several burly men to lift, because there are few forces in Nature more powerful than a woman who needs to rearrange furniture. It would not surprise me to wake up one morning and find that we lived in an entirely different house.

(I realize that I'm making gender-based generalizations here, but my feeling is that if God did not want us to make gender-based generalizations, She would not have given us genders.)

GUYS LIKE A REALLY POINTLESS CHALLENGE.

Not long ago I was sitting in my office at the *Miami Herald*'s Sunday magazine, *Tropic*, reading my fan mail[4],

---

[4] Typical fan letter: "Who cuts your hair? Beavers?"

when I heard several of my guy co-workers in the hall-way talking about how fast they could run the forty-yard dash. These are guys in their thirties and forties who work in journalism, where the most demanding physical requirement is the ability to digest vending-machine food. In other words, these guys have absolutely no need to run the forty-yard dash.

But one of them, Mike Wilson, was writing a story about a star high-school football player who could run it in 4.38 seconds. Now if Mike had written a story about, say, a star high-school poet, none of my guy co-workers would have suddenly decided to find out how well they could write sonnets. But when Mike turned in his story, they became *deeply* concerned about how fast they could run the forty-yard dash. They were so concerned that the magazine's editor, Tom Shroder, decided that they should get a stopwatch and go out to a nearby park and find out. Which they did, a bunch of guys taking off their shoes and running around barefoot in a public park on company time.

This is what I heard them talking about, out in the hall. I heard Tom, who was thirty-eight years old, saying that his time in the forty had been 5.75 seconds. And I thought to myself: "This is ridiculous. These are middle-aged guys, supposedly adults, and they're out there *bragging* about their performance in this stupid, juvenile footrace." Finally I couldn't stand it anymore.

"Hey!" I shouted. "*I* could beat 5.75 seconds."

So we went out to the park and measured off forty yards, and the guys told me that I had three chances to make my best time. On the first try my time was 5.78 seconds, just three-hundredths of a second slower than Tom's, even though, at forty-five, I was seven years older than he. So I just *knew* I'd beat him on the second attempt if I ran really, really hard, which I did for a solid ten yards, at which point my left hamstring muscle, which had not yet shifted into Sprint Mode from Mail-Reading Mode, went, and I quote, "pop."

I had to be helped off the field. I was in considerable pain, and I was obviously not going to be able to walk right for weeks. I felt pretty stupid. Fortunately, Beth was sympathetic.

"You *idiot*," she sympathized. "What on earth did you

think was going to happen? You're forty-five years old! You didn't even warm up!"

She didn't understand. But the guys in my office did, especially Tom, who took the time to call me at home, where I was sitting with an ice pack on my leg and twenty-three Advil in my bloodstream, so he could express his concern.

"Just remember," he said. *"You didn't beat my time."*

There are countless other examples of guys rising to meet pointless challenges. Virtually all sports fall into this category, as well as a large part of U.S. foreign policy. ("I'll bet you can't capture Manuel Noriega!" "Oh YEAH??")

GUYS DO NOT HAVE A RIGID AND WELL-DEFINED MORAL CODE.

This is not the same as saying that guys are bad. Guys *are* capable of doing bad things, but this generally happens when they try to be Men and start becoming manly and aggressive and stupid. When they're being just plain guys, they aren't so much actively *evil* as they are *lost*. Because guys have never really grasped the Basic Human Moral Code, which I believe was invented by women millions of years ago when all the guys were out engaging in some other activity, such as seeing who could burp the loudest. When they came back, there were certain rules that they were expected to follow unless they wanted to get into Big Trouble, and they have been trying to follow these rules ever since, with extremely irregular results. Because guys have never *internalized* these rules. Guys are similar to my small auxiliary backup dog, Zippy, a guy dog[5] who has been told numerous times that he is NOT supposed to (1) get into the kitchen garbage or (2) poop on the floor. He knows that these are the rules, but he has never really understood *why*, and sometimes he gets to thinking: Sure, they *ordinarily* don't want me getting into the garbage, but obviously this rule is not meant to apply when there are certain extenuat-

---

[5] We also have a female dog, Earnest, who *never* breaks the rules.

ing[6] circumstances, such as (1) they just threw away some perfectly good seven-week-old Kung Pao Chicken, and (2) they are not home.

And so when we come home, our kitchen floor has been transformed into GarbageFest USA, and Zippy, who usually comes rushing up to greet us, is off in a corner disguised in a wig and sunglasses, hoping to get into the Federal Bad Dog Relocation Program before we discover the scene of the crime.

When we yell at him, he frequently becomes so upset that he poops on the floor.

Morally, most guys are just like Zippy, only taller and usually less hairy. Guys are *aware* of the rules of moral behavior, but they have trouble keeping these rules in the forefronts of their minds at certain times, especially the present. This is especially true in the area of faithfulness to one's mate. I realize, of course, that there are countless examples of guys being faithful to their mates until they die, usually as a result of being eaten by their mates immediately following copulation. Guys outside of the spider community, however, do not have a terrific record of faithfulness.

I'm not saying guys are scum. I'm saying that many guys who consider themselves to be committed to their marriages will stray if they are confronted with overwhelming temptation, defined as "virtually any temptation."

OK, so maybe I *am* saying guys are scum. But they're not *mean-spirited* scum. And few of them—even when they are out of town on business trips, far from their wives, and have a clear-cut opportunity—will poop on the floor.

GUYS ARE NOT GREAT AT COMMUNICATING THEIR INTIMATE FEELINGS, ASSUMING THEY HAVE ANY.

This is an aspect of guyhood that is very frustrating to women in general, and my wife in particular. I'll be reading the newspaper, and the phone will ring; I'll answer

[6] I am taking some liberties here with Zippy's vocabulary. More likely, in his mind, he uses the term "mitigating."

it, listen for ten minutes, hang up, and resume reading. Finally Beth will say: "Who was that?"

And I'll say: "Phil Wonkerman's mom."

(Phil is an old friend we haven't heard from in seventeen years.)

And Beth will say, "Well?"

And I'll say, "Well what?"

And Beth will say, "What did she *say*?"

And I'll say, "She said Phil is fine," making it clear by my tone of voice that, although I do not wish to be rude, I AM trying to read the newspaper here, and I happen to be right in the middle of an important panel of Calvin and Hobbes.

But Beth, ignoring this, will say, "That's ALL she said?"

And she will not let up. She will continue to ask district-attorney-style questions, forcing me to recount the conversation until she's satisfied that she has the entire story, which is that Phil just got out of prison after serving a sentence for a murder he committed when he became a drug addict because of the guilt he felt when his wife died in a freak submarine accident while Phil was having an affair with a nun, but now he's all straightened out and has a good job as a trapeze artist and is almost through with the surgical part of his sex change and recently became happily engaged to marry a prominent member of the Grateful Dead, so in other words he is fine, which is EXACTLY what I told Beth in the first place, but is that enough? No. She wants to hear *every single detail*.

We have some good friends, Buzz and Libby, whom we see about twice a year. When we get together, Beth and Libby always wind up in a conversation, lasting several days, during which they discuss virtually every significant event that has occurred in their lives and the lives of those they care about, sharing their innermost thoughts, analyzing and probing, inevitably coming to a deeper understanding of each other, and a strengthening of a cherished friendship. Whereas Buzz and I watch the playoffs.

This is not to say Buzz and I don't share our feelings. Sometimes we get quite emotional.

"That's not a FOUL??" one of us will say.

Or: "YOU'RE TELLING ME THAT'S NOT A FOUL???"

I don't mean to suggest that all we talk about is sports. We also discuss, openly and without shame, what kind of pizza we need to order. We have a fine time together, but we don't have heavy conversations, and sometimes, after the visit is over, I'm surprised to learn—from Beth, who learned it from Libby—that there has recently been some new wrinkle in Buzz's life, such as that he now has an artificial leg.

(For the record, Buzz does NOT have an artificial leg. At least he didn't mention anything about it to me.)

I have another good friend, Gene, and one time, when he was going through a major medical development in his life, our families spent a weekend together. During this time Gene and I talked a lot and enjoyed each other's company immensely, but—this is true—the most intimate personal statement he made to me is that he has reached Level 24 of a video game called "Arkanoid." He had even seen the Evil Presence, although he refused to tell me what it looks like. We're very close, but there is a limit.

You may think that my friends and I are Neanderthals, and that a lot of guys are different. This is true. A lot of guys don't use words at *all*. They communicate entirely by nonverbal methods, such as sharing bait.